# CREATE FOREVER TEAMMATES

ELITE PERFORMANCE

KT

TOO-E

ptouhey@eliteperformancetoo-e.com
574-360-9188.
eliteperformancetoo-e.com

ISBN: 978-1-7379762-0-2 (print)
ISBN: 978-1-7379762-1-9 (ebook)

Ordering Information:
Special discounts are available on quantity purchases by corporations, associations, and others. For details, contact ptouhey@eliteperformancetoo-e.com or go to eliteperformancetoo-e.com

# CREATE FOREVER TEAMMATES

How Connections and Relationships
Are the Winning Steps in Life and Sports

**PATRICK TOUHEY**

# FOREWORD
## CULTURE TRUMPS STRATEGY

In 2011, I became the athletic director at Denison University, my alma mater, and was tasked to lead a strong and flourishing program. I'd spent many years of my life preparing for this new opportunity, and was confident that my experience as a coach and teacher at two very strong liberal arts institutions would be enough to overcome any challenges I might face.

Early on, it became apparent that some of our student-athletes weren't enjoying their experience. At the time, we were working hard to develop our core competencies and define success despite being in an era where the external audience only saw our wins and losses. Our goal was to create an environment where our student athletes could grow academically, athletically, and socially. While that might sound simple, it's actually very complex work.

Winning and success are important without a doubt, but anyone who has competed in college athletics knows that it is the relationships you remember most. This is why it was imperative for us to create a space that was conducive for relationship, individual, and team development so that our students could achieve what we perceive to be the ultimate success in college athletics.

With some of the issues that were popping up at the university, I decided we could use an outside resource to help us accomplish our goals. Once I had the opportunity to meet Kevin Touhey and read his books, I hired him to help me lead the division. I wanted him to take a deep dive into our programs and aid those teams who might need more hands-on work building team culture.

For many years, Kevin was a big part of the Denison family and remains so to this day despite his untimely loss to cancer. While this loss was a heavy one to bear, little did I know that Kevin was helping his brother Patrick to develop his intellectual material in the cultural development space.

After several years of getting to know Patrick, I hired him to continue the work we started with Kevin to identify teams within our programs that had existing challenges developing team culture. Patrick traveled to the small village of Granville on glorious fall days, bitter-cold wintery days, and in the Ohio chilly days of spring. While not everyone loves self-reflection or develops habits of self-awareness in an effort to grow, those who lead understand the importance of this work.

Patrick's book is a testimony of how walking into the space of vulnerability, we learn the skills necessary for self-growth throughout one's lifetime. Patrick uses the platform of sport to help facilitate the growth and development of life skills. His writing is real, poignant, vulnerable and inspired.

Patrick is the "real deal" and utilizes his life's experiences to develop workshops to help others grow, individually and collectively.

I applaud his writing and plan to continue to "team up" with Patrick as my leadership work unfolds.

But above all else, I'd like to thank you, Patrick, for your vulnerability, honesty, and integrity in building your leadership-development workshops. And to all the readers, I hope you enjoy this book, get real, and continue to embrace a growth mindset for life!

Nan Carney-DeBord
Associate Vice President of Athletics and Recreation
Denison University

# TABLE OF CONTENTS

# CONTENT WARNING

This book contains language pertaining to topics such as alcohol, drugs, suicide, cancer, suicidal ideation, anxiety, death, depression, addiction, disordered eating, homophobia, abortion, self-harm, and racism.

# DISCLAIMER

This book is a work of creative nonfiction. I have reconstructed and portrayed the characters and events to the best of my memory and ability. While all the stories and events in this book are true, some names and identifying details have been changed to protect the privacy of the people involved. Also, because no conversations can be remembered word for word verbatim, the basis of the dialogues in all instances are accurate and have been retold to capture and express the concepts, feelings, and emotions.

# CHAPTER ONE

# THE SPORTS EPIDEMIC

I remember what it took to get a game of basketball going when I was a kid.

First, I would call George to start the chain reaction. George would call Jerry, Jerry would call Ethan, Ethan would call Tim, and so on, until a herd of us gathered through telephone lines.

Whenever I told my parents what I was going to do, their reactions weren't full of fear or anxiety about potential dangers or injuries. Instead, they would offer a simple, "Have fun!" as I walked out the door.

And with that first gust of fresh air, excitement began coursing through my veins. I was on the precipice of independence, imagination, and joy, impatient to play my favorite sport with people I loved.

Most of the time walking wasn't quick enough, so I'd run around the corner and sprint down a few streets, collecting friends as I went and only slowing down when we reached our destination at the corner of Penn Avenue and Sixth Street. All together, we headed toward the court side by side, jabbering about who was going to be on each team and who the best players were.

It all came with a feeling of endless possibilities, the excitement bursting from the cacophony of our voices. There was chaos as we constantly cut off one another, switching subjects that ranged from what kind of mischief we were going to get into later that day to our dreams of going pro until eventually we reached the court and pretended we actually were.

These pick-up games that were formed became the vehicle through which we found ourselves. We had to choose teams, be leaders and listeners, practice decision-making, and handle the disappointment when you were the last one chosen. And when the ball was picked up and we started to play, there was strategic thinking, competition, and more dreaming as we imitated the greats like Jerry West, Clyde Frazier, and Bill Russel.

We made all of this happen without ever getting our parents involved. Maybe this is something you can relate to, or maybe you're just someone who *recognizes we have a big problem with the way sports are played today.*

Due to the lack of integrating spirit, fun, and excitement, the overall experience of playing sports is similar to having a job for a large corporation. The student-athletes take orders from the big man, play specialized roles, and create a product that's called *winning.* Everything is run by adults, and instead of kids being forced to figure it out themselves, coaches organize drills and teach techniques while parents watch their child intently and yell out corrections from the sideline. In every facet, adults are interjected into the experience until it becomes about *us* instead of them. And it's this adult overinvolvement that's leaving this generation wounded.

Maybe that's why student athletes quit their sport at such high rates in college. Brown University recently reported that 30% of athletes quit their respective teams in 2016.[1] Harvard relayed a similar statistic with a one in four dropout rate, with many former student athletes citing "injuries, mental health concerns, academic and extracurricular interests, and a diminished love for their sport" as their reason for leaving.[2] Maybe that's why it's documented that student-athletes binge drink at higher rates compared to other students on campus, with one in five male student-athletes intaking more than 10 drinks in an outing.[3]

This could also be a sufficient way to explain why high school athletes' abuse of prescription painkillers is on the rise,[4] the increased struggles with anxiety and depression over the years,[5] and why eating disorders affect up to 62% of females and 33% of males in weight-class and aesthetic sports.[6]

Needless to say, we have a huge problem on our hands, and it's about time we do something about it.

***

In 2016, my brother Kevin passed away from lung cancer. When he died, he left behind his wife, two young children, and his incredibly important work. I saw him for the last time in his living room, which he'd converted into his bedroom. I'd flown out to New Jersey to spend a final few days with him, and so that we could talk alone face to face.

My brother was in the worst shape I'd ever seen him. His face was pale, his body was skeletal, and his clothes barely hung on his back. It was hard to see him this way, as my big brother was always someone who was larger than life to me. Seeing him stuck in bed was another painful reminder of his condition—a stark contrast to the athlete and coach he'd always been. Thankfully, this didn't stop him from smiling when I walked in the room.

"Hey, Kev," I let out.

"You're not looking too good," he joked.

Though it was hard, I forced a laugh and cracked back at him. "Says you."

As I moved closer to him, I noticed how blue his eyes were. It was like nothing I'd ever seen before. They were so clear and bright, almost like you could see right through them. That was how I knew my brother was in a place of purity—without an agenda or motive.

Being in the presence of someone in this state is extremely powerful, and I felt something special, maybe even divine, in the air. I knelt beside him and he took my hand. The second he did, tears rolled down my face. Our conversation covered topics we didn't want to leave unsaid, but it ended with a question—a question that was going to change my life and the lives of others forever.

"Will you promise to continue my work?"

Kevin's work was and still is hard to describe. On the surface, Elite Performance Too-E is a program that helps coaches and players build a connection so they can function better as a team. Kevin dreamt up the company in 2004 to specifically aid high school and college-level sports teams as well as some corporations and individuals. But underneath all of this, Elite Performance Too-E is so much more. It's about teaching and motivating with passion, purpose, integrity, and love in an athletic world that runs primarily on outcomes, wins, and points. But most of all, it's about awakening athletes to the responsibility they must build and protect relationships with each other.

The byproduct of Elite Performance Too-E's investment in a program is developing a family that has a heightened degree of trust, confidence, mental toughness, and intimate connections while also showing support for each other during real-life difficulties and struggles. Since its conception, Elite Performance Too-E has contributed to the success of high school sports teams that have won state championships and college-level programs that rank in the top 20 nationally. On an individual level, Elite Performance Too-E has helped produce strong leaders that achieve the highest level of recognition in their sport and get those athletes who were completely burnt out back on track by reestablishing their passions. In the corporate arena, Elite Performance Too-E has also facilitated the identification of the distractions, obstacles, and blocks that were holding officers, managers, and employees back from performing at their highest possible level.

Even though Kevin believed I held the empathy and compassion to do this kind of work, I was still nowhere near the right headspace to be doing it. I felt that way because I knew what it took for Kevin to do this job the way he did.

Kevin told me once he always took a few moments to be by himself before his sessions. This was part of his ritual. And every time he did, he would say in prayer, *give me the strength to get out of the way.* In this line of work, you can't have an agenda, ego, or ulterior motive. You're standing in front of a crowd of people, attempting to express concern and care for them in hopes that it will help them become the best version of themselves.

To do that, you need to be fully present, healthy, and available—all things I was not.

And based on my history, I wasn't a likely contender to be those things any time soon. By that time in my life, I had been an alcoholic, had a panic and anxiety disorder, and come close to committing suicide twice.

When I was sitting down with my brother in his home, even though I had overcome my past and had crafted a life for myself that looked great on paper—a successful business owner, father to two wonderful children, and a happily married man—I couldn't shake a feeling of emptiness that haunted me.

How was I anyone to look up to? How could someone like me provide for these kids?

*How can I do this without you?*

I know Kevin sensed this hole inside of me. He had a talent for seeing past facades. Growing up in abject poverty with a drunk, abusive father will leave you with scars. I was one of the youngest of ten siblings, and we were constantly walking on eggshells in homes that we'd eventually be evicted from, living off meals bought with food stamps.

That dark voice inside my head was passed down to me from my father. He projected his insecurities, fear, dysfunction, and alcoholism onto us. Every day it was, *you will amount to nothing, you're worth nothing,* or *you don't deserve anything* on repeat. It was a record that we couldn't stop. And when you hear these things repeatedly, you start to believe them.

During those tough times, athletics were a ray of light. Kevin, the oldest of the boys in the family, was a star basketball player, and his successes on the court gave us something to be excited about in a chaotic home environment. His accomplishments in basketball ultimately carried him to college, where he graduated with the first degree in our family.

Kevin went on to become a coach for a collegiate NAIA program—a program that he tried to get me to join several times, even though I could never fully commit because of my alcoholism. He was eventually able to bring me on as his assistant coach, which put me on a redeeming path. If Kevin hadn't done that, I probably wouldn't be here today.

Athletics saved me back then, so maybe he thought it could save me again.

At that point, I'd come to a few sessions of his that were focused on showing athletes the bigger picture, building connection amongst teammates, and living with integrity. I was content with chiming in here and there, but I didn't have the courage to do it alone. He was asking me to take on something that was truly his heart, soul, and every breath.

It was like he was asking me to replace him, but I could never. No one could.

Still, it only took me two minutes to accept. What I didn't realize at the time was saying yes would be the easy part.

## Our Mission

Instead of being primarily focused on fun, today's youth sports are weighted toward outcomes and results, the *extrinsic* parts of the game. In our experience at Elite Performance Too-E, we have found that hyper-focusing on extrinsic goals and commitments creates a culture with elements of stress, emptiness, selfishness—a continuing list that gets bigger by the day.

In this type of environment, the players no longer think about what they can do for each other and tend to care only about their individual success instead (What's in it for me? How do I set myself up for my future? How will I be recognized?).

Kevin became aware of this shift in attitude and the emotional toll it took on players during his time as an assistant coach at the University of Pennsylvania, which caused him to abandon his pursuit of being a Division I (D1) head basketball coach and help young athletes on a much larger scale. This pointed him in the direction of developing what would eventually become Elite Performance Too-E.

Our focus with Elite Performance Too-E is to help teams cultivate *the intrinsic*, which includes building relationships, trust, and values. Doing so, as I have seen time and time again, dramatically improves a team's performance *and* the players' emotional health.

The tenants that Kevin developed and that I continue to teach are what I hope to help you discover. With these principles in your toolbox, you'll then be able to help players reach their fullest potential—as an athlete and as a person. Just as my brother's philosophies changed my life, I hope this book changes your life and the lives of those around you forever.

# CHAPTER TWO

# VULNERABILITY

## TEARING DOWN THE WALL

Shortly after Kevin's passing, I quickly realized it was time for the work to begin. Specifically, Kevin had asked me to reach out to the Shawnee High School football program, a client that was very near and dear to his heart, to continue his work there. A week later, I found myself standing in front of roughly 50 players and the entire coaching staff.

I clenched my hands together to hide the trembling and did my best to control my breathing. That's when the doubt that I wouldn't be able to live up to his work snuck in. I was filled with the fear that I was going to be considered a failure and would ruin the lives of all those people who needed help. At the time I remember thinking, *What the hell did I get myself into?*

On the verge of a panic attack, I asked Kevin to help me. *Kevin, I said, if you're there, please give me strength, courage, and guidance. Please help me find the way to be authentic, genuine, and loving like you always were. I need your help to find the words, the way to connect with these people.*

Miraculously, what I heard back was, *Show vulnerability, Patrick.* Confidence replaced my anxiety, and I suddenly knew what I had to do. The first thing I said was, "I miss my brother so much," and then surprisingly everything else began to pour out of me like water. I continued to share that I was still very much grieving his death and afraid that I would let him down. I told them about the insecurities and shortcomings I had that I feared would prevent me from doing his work.

When I was done talking, I felt a soothing peace come over me. I had confidence that my brother was with me. I knew that by being vulnerable, I had let go of the idea that I had to be perfect, and unexpectedly, the session just began to take its own course. When I was done, I received a standing ovation, and the entire coaching staff came over to tell me that Kevin would have been so very proud of me.

I would love to tell you that I never struggled with doubt or whether I was enough to do Kevin's work from that point forward, but that was not the case. Instead, I focused on being as vulnerable as I needed to be in every session and continued to pray to Kevin when I was at his house, which is where I would stay when doing workshops for Shawnee and Lenape High School.

But one evening as I knelt with my head down, I sensed that something was different. I felt Kevin's presence in a way I never had before and heard him say, "Patrick, I am so proud of you, and I love you so very much. Remember, this is our work Patrick—not my work."

I interpreted this as a gentle reminder from my brother that he didn't ask me to be him—he only asked me to continue the work he started. He believed that I could teach the lessons from a place of my *own* experience, strength, wisdom, and hope, and that I already possessed everything I needed within me to teach his lessons.

What I know today is that I bring Kevin with me to every session. Not with the worry of letting him down, but with the great comfort and confidence that he stands next to me to cheer me on, love me, and express his gratitude that I continue with his legacy in my own way.

This is the beautiful gift that vulnerability gave me.

Kevin used to refer to the word "intimacy" as "into-me-see," meaning, *enter my heart and soul, know my fears and loves.* He believed that many of the decisions or actions we take, when peeled to their core, come from a place of fear or love.

I happen to agree with that theory.

When a coaching staff strategizes for the upcoming season, vulnerability is likely the last thing they plug into their action plan. This is likely because vulnerability and sports don't traditionally go together and are sometimes thought of as a sign of weakness. It's also just as true that most coaching staffs simply have no idea how to go about teaching it.

However, if this intrinsic skill is never brought to the forefront, a team will never reach its fullest potential. Without it, they won't be able to develop a high degree of trust, build confidence in each other, and believe in themselves as a unit—which are all crucial elements when working toward achieving the ultimate level of success.

## The Panthers' Sessions

Winning was not this team's problem.

They were a championship-level group that produced star athletes, achieved many NCAA accolades, and had a coach in the NCAA Basketball Hall of Fame. Though all those things are true, the team needed a serious attitude adjustment. Year in and year out, they were the team with the highest number of violations, ranging from destruction of property to disorderly conduct. Every game they won meant another night of celebrating, and that meant there was always potential for more trouble.

Even worse, the fan base in the student section were a parallel version of the players. I remember hearing them shout nasty remarks at the opposing players' appearances, their worth, and even personal remarks about their families and girlfriends. The point is, this team attracted *that* kind of energy, and it was a big problem.

Then one Thursday afternoon, the phone rang. It was the athletic director of the university who had previously hired Kevin to work with several of their athletic teams and coaches. He'd become aware of the work I was doing with Elite Performance Too-E through social media. The comments and responses made by the coaches about their teams' significant improvement as players and people were similar to the results he saw in his program as a result of Kevin's work, so he decided to reach out to me.

He explained that the team needed a serious cultural overhaul and talked to me about some of their problems. The fact that they led all athletics teams for the number of violations reported (well over 100) is what stood out to me the most.

When I accepted the assignment, the athletic director left me with a single sentiment: "All I can tell you is good luck."

This was hardly reassuring. Even though I knew this job would be a challenge, I was excited to begin. This was one of the schools where Kevin had hoped I would continue his work. Even though it took two years after his passing, his wish would be granted, and I knew he was looking down at me with a big smile on his face.

I was the enemy when I first walked into their locker room.

Perhaps I represented something inaccessible and untouchable, like the feelings these players desperately wanted to ignore. Not very long into our first session, I knew they had a serious problem with trusting each other—which, unfortunately, isn't surprising in this line of work. I could see it right away in their tense, rigid, and disengaged body language when teammates spoke. It became obvious that there was friction, but no one was willing to put any of it on the table. This lack of honesty told me trust within the team hadn't been developed.

I knew I needed to work with this group on embracing vulnerability, and that it wouldn't be easy. The level of discomfort and anxiety associated with letting a wall down can be overwhelming, especially for young athletes who've been taught to push through adversity at any cost.

To try and overcome this obstacle, I decided to start by sharing something about myself.

"I'm Patrick Touhey," I said. "The founder of a multimillion-dollar company, a successful basketball coach and life coach, and a happily married man with two beautiful adult children."

I paused, then continued.

"I am also Patrick Touhey, a recovering alcoholic of over 30 years, who grew up in poverty, who was raised in a mentally and physically abusive household, who had a panic and anxiety disorder, who has bouts of depression, and who came close to taking my own life—twice."

There was dead silence in the room. I looked around and observed the players' body language. I witnessed the shock of some over a stranger sharing something so personal. I saw empathy in the eyes of others, and I took note of the ones that were on the verge of raising their hands and speaking up but feared to do so.

"Would anyone like to share something with their teammates about themselves?" I was met only with the same silence as before. Instead of ending this though, I forced everyone to sit and allow it to be uncomfortable. Over the years, I have come to understand the power of letting silence run its course. That was something Kevin taught me.

I decided to interject once more to inform them that it didn't have to be anything intense or painful. More silence, more discomfort. Of course, I knew what they were thinking. Sharing something so deep and personal would indicate to others that they don't have it all together, and that would be a sign of weakness.

Finally, I said, "I understand that being open isn't easy, but it doesn't have to be perfect. *You* don't have to be perfect."

A single player lifted his head from the floor to meet mine. He tentatively raised his hand and asked if I would be willing to tell them more about wanting to commit suicide. I immediately sensed the pain and hopelessness in this young man's eyes. Sometimes, sharing your story can save others, so I did.

The year was 2009. I'd just sold my company for a great deal of money and achieved a high level of prosperity, despite growing up in a house where I'd been told I would amount to nothing. I had proved my dad wrong and was the happiest I'd ever been.

Unfortunately, that feeling would be short-lived.

My identity, self-worth, and confidence were embedded in my relationship with my company. As a result, after I sold it, I couldn't help feeling like I was undeserving of happiness unless I achieved something else. I had all the money I would ever need, but for the next two years I went through severe bouts of intense anxiety, panic attacks, and depression. I envisioned myself in this black hole, shaking, afraid, and alone—and it disgusted me.

Still, I kept it to myself and pretended I was fine.

One day, before the sun rose, I was jolted awake. My heart raced and a cold sweat dripped down my face. I was having a major panic attack and looked over at my wife sleeping peacefully next to me with the thought of waking her for help. I reached out to touch her but stopped an inch away, knowing there was nothing she could do to relieve my pain and anguish.

As I headed for the medicine cabinet, I glanced at myself in the mirror and saw a man who was emotionally, physically, and spiritually beaten. I gathered all the sleeping pills, Xanax, and antidepressants that had been prescribed to me over the years and went down the stairs, grabbed my car keys, and got into my car.

I planned to drive to a remote location and take all these pills I had in my hands.

Before I could get out of the driveway, I paused, looked down at all the pills, then up at my house where my wife and kids were sleeping. During my darkest moments, it was always the thought of them that kept me from committing suicide, and it was what saved me then.

I turned the car off and walked back into the house. When my wife woke up, I told her I needed to go to the hospital because I was afraid I would end my life if I didn't. Shortly after, I voluntarily checked into the psychiatric floor at Elkhart General Hospital and got the help I needed.

As I was speaking, I saw there were tears in some of the players' eyes. Guessing by how thick their emotional walls had been, these tears for some were probably the first in years. Others were squirming in their chairs from the discomfort, while others dropped their head to hide what they felt.

We sat like this for a long time, allowing each person to process what I'd said in their own way. Eventually, one of the players raised his hand and asked if he could share something. He went on to talk about his struggle with self-worth. He'd got involved with drugs and made poor decisions. He related that he often felt stupid and was incapable of obtaining success. To me, this young man was very courageous. And by taking this risk, he gave other teammates the permission needed to speak up.

By the time we finished that day, nearly 10 players had shared their stories. Each person received empathy, support, and love from their teammates. It was an incredible sight to watch, and I was proud to be a part of it. As always, some chose not to speak, but I know they walked out of the session aware that they're not alone—and there's great power in that.

At the end of the session everyone funneled out, but one player stayed behind. It was the same one who asked me to share my story. He thanked me and explained that he'd been struggling with suicidal thoughts. My story gave him hope that the negative thoughts would subside. Over the course of that season, he was able to receive the assistance he needed and regained his mental and emotional health.

Since that first session, the Panthers have grown immensely. After spending two and a half seasons with them, the number of reported incidents decreased from more than 100 to single digits, and their cumulative GPA skyrocketed to over 3.0—a program record.

And most importantly of all, the Panthers began to see that vulnerability is a strength and not a weakness. As a result, their trust in each other grew to an unprecedented level.

## Fostering the Connection

Obtaining and executing vulnerability pays off with huge dividends on the field or court. But even more importantly is how it can pay off in everyday life. To create the kind of environment that allows for trust-building, a program must first be willing to take time away from practice to teach the skill. Then, the facilitator of the conversation must set ground rules by introducing these concepts:

- Non-judgment

- Empathetic listening

- Embracing discomfort

- Welcoming all perspectives and realities

These skills are difficult to pick up and maintain, but the mediator of the conversation can point out times when the team strays beyond these guardrails, and in doing so, will teach the athletes about them.

During the workshops at Elite Performance Too-E, we've found that a great way to get the conversation rolling is by either sharing a story that requires vulnerability or by completing an exercise. The secret sauce for a successful session is that the players must be *engaged*. Here's an example of one of the exercises we do:

1. Write a list of 25 words such as jealousy, hate, and selfishness on a whiteboard and call them *distractions*. It's important to call them this because a distraction is less judgmental, and judgments will kill vulnerability.

2. Next, break the team into small groups of three to five and ask that they work together to select 12 words that affect the family the most.

3. After giving them a few minutes, quiet the room and ask each group, one at a time, what their top 12 words were.

4. After each group has gone, narrow the list from 25 down to the 12 most selected words.

5. Then, follow up by having the group vote anonymously on their top six words. Later, ask the group why they think those six top words are the most important at the end of the process.

This exercise is great because it encourages discourse and requires the team to discuss their faults. Essentially, it allows them to practice vulnerability without ever saying the word. At times, the discussion can become heated when players disagree or try to tell each other how to feel. Usually, I try not to get involved because there's power in letting those emotions run their course. However, if it becomes unproductive, I will step in and remind the players that they need to be empathetic listeners and ask for permission to give feedback instead of just throwing it out there.

Finally, I ask the players to give some personal examples about times they have exemplified the words on the boards. It can be discomforting for coaches and teammates alike, but the payoff is incredible. Typically, one or two brave players will share a story, which permits others to open up.

Asking open-ended questions that start a discussion is another great way to introduce vulnerability. Here are some of the questions I like to ask:

- When hearing the word "vulnerability," what's your initial reaction? What's your understanding of its meaning?

- What benefits, if any, can come from embracing and executing vulnerability within a team?

- What pitfalls can arise from embracing and executing vulnerability within a team?

- Have any of you displayed vulnerability within a relationship? If so, what effect did it have on the relationship?

- If I were to tell you that embracing vulnerability within this team would escalate your level of athletic performance, what skill set would be required for this team to even just entertain allowing vulnerable communication?

- When was there a time you failed your teammate, on or off the court/field?

- If I were to setup a space that would allow you to honestly express the shortcomings you have as a person and player without judgement, what would those shortcomings consist of?

- What holds you back from being vulnerable?

- What is it about yourself that restricts you from being the best possible version of yourself?

Some will initially be uncomfortable with these sessions and may retaliate with attitude. Nonetheless, it's important to not force anyone. It must come naturally and at the right time, and that may be different for each person.

Also, be aware that getting 14- to 22-year-old athletes to express vulnerability is challenging. A fear of being flawed may hold them back from being vulnerable. Having said that, I fully believe in the strength vulnerability brings and can tell you that it's a powerful tool for success on and off the court.

## The Heart of a Team

Vulnerability is one of the many factors required to build your team's collective heart. It nurtures trust, and a team needs trust to succeed. When this connection is achieved, the results can be incredible and miracles will happen.

I spent an afternoon with my brother back in 2010 studying a Division I college team that had efficiently integrated vulnerability into their program. We were told to watch the first 40 minutes of practice where the players coach each other. Immediately intrigued, my brother and I walked into the blaring sun with squinted eyes and laid our sights on the football field.

To our amazement, you would've thought there were a thousand coaches watching because of how they were playing. Wide receivers were darting around defenses, drills were being run by freshmen, and stats were being taken by seniors. And all of this was happening amongst the euphony of high fives and laughter.

At one point, Kevin and I watched a quarterback drill where a ball was thrown at least 15 feet over the receiver's head. Without another second to waste, both players darted off the field and dropped into pushups. We were stunned.

I ran up to the receiver and asked, "Why are you doing that?"

He finished his set, got up to his feet, and brushed the dirt off his palms. "I should've caught that." He stated this confidently, as if it was a fact.

"But that was way over your head."

"It doesn't matter. I should've caught that," he replied. He pointed to the quarterback, who was just finishing up his set. "He's telling me, 'I'm sorry' with those pushups. That's what teammates do."

Because I was still learning at that point, I asked my brother why he thought this team acted that way. He told me that it was all about their connection. They loved each other unconditionally, even when someone screwed up, and were fighting for each other—not just to win. That kind of fighting requires love and trust.

This is when it clicked for me. I was reminded of the time I spent on the basketball court with my buddies back in the day. It may have been many years apart and in a different age, but this team and my team weren't all that different. This is how sports were meant to be played.

# CHAPTER THREE

# COMPASSION
## THE FEAR BUSTER

Jim Harbaugh, the head football coach at the University of Michigan, will sometimes motivate his players by shouting at the top of his lungs, "Who has it better than us?"*

*And his players always respond, "Nobody!" Here's why.

We all know that fear can severely limit an athlete's potential and capabilities, but this isn't fear of the other team or competition.

It's the fear of failing.

Many players have a difficult time recovering from a failed play or from delivering a less than desirable result. For both coaches and players, it's not easy to resolve this problem. This mindset is likely rooted in how we teach athletes. From a young age, they're exposed to passionate parents, judgment from trainers, private lessons, nonstop practices, intense coaches—the list goes on and on.

*https://www.youtube.com/watch?v=hLwEuYcibSM

This type of socialization can only lead to a fear-based mentality, as an immense amount of importance is placed on perfection.

In turn, this teaches and reinforces destructive habitual responses when experiencing failure. This way of thinking is extremely detrimental, not only for the athlete's mental health, but also for their athletic performance. The individual will choose safe plays over rewarding ones and be thwarted by mental limitations. Emotionally, they'll protect themselves from future embarrassment by pretending not to care. I believe this mentality has driven many to not even try.

Still not convinced that this coaching style is unproductive?

Let's imagine that a player does succeed. But because they're primarily driven by fear, the athlete will experience more mental, emotional, spiritual, and physical drain than joy, leading to burnout. Eventually they'll quit before they can reach their full potential.

Remember that players are human before they're athletes. This means they're folly to the hurdles we all deal with every day, *with* the added weight of having to perform under extreme amounts of pressure. I watch these athletes play day after day out of fear—erring on the side of caution rather than basking in the joy of the game—and it saddens me to see them formulating protective mechanisms to avoid disappointment, struggle, and uncomfortable emotions at such a young age.

And it's indeed a problem that requires a solution.

From my perspective, self-compassion is the answer. So, what's self-compassion exactly? It's not the title of a self-help book, and it's not about letting your players off the hook. At its core, self-compassion is an unconditional love for oneself. And in the case of failure, self-compassion grants the knowledge that, in the process of stretching or sharpening ourselves, mistakes are inevitable. That every error is something to get excited about because it's an opportunity to grow. Successes should still be celebrated, but it's often failed attempts that are the catalyst to mastery. When you approach sport and competition with this mindset, it can be empowering.

But in order for self-compassion to thrive, the right kind of environment must be built. This might include an atmosphere where mistakes are put in the proper perspective and language is used that reminds athletes that failing is a tremendous experience. You might also have a metaphorical or literal sign in the locker room that says, "Did you fail today? Awesome! Make sure to thank it. Why? Because it's time to learn and grow."

When players learn self-compassion, they begin to understand that their screw up on the court or field doesn't mean that *they are a failure*. After this truth is ingrained in them, they respond better to criticism and overcome the negative self-talk they've built up over the years. They have more energy and passion and persevere whenever they struggle. Time and time again, I've seen that the players, coaches, and teams who execute this skill reach goals that exceed expectations because it ignites a belief that anything is possible.

Teaching this skill starts with the language and philosophy a program uses when talking about the big f-word: failure.

First, leaders should ask this question to understand how players usually respond to disappointment. *What's your internal dialogue when you fail or don't do something perfectly?* Note the athlete's response. Do they beat themselves up? Do they blame others? Do they try to rationalize why they messed up? Do they see themselves as uncoachable? Do they act out in self-sabotaging ways?

If the answer to any of these questions is yes, internal restructuring will be needed.

Teach them that the initial response to failure should be *curiosity*, allowing one to search for the reason why the letdown occurred. Reactions such as disappointment, frustration, and anger are understandably second nature, but the sooner we let go of those unhelpful emotions and replace them with interest, then the occurrence becomes just another learning experience.

Reassure them of this every time a mistake is made.

Curiosity is also crucial because it will open a player's introspection. To learn why they made a mistake, they'll have to search inside of themselves, and in doing so will open their minds to change and growth in all aspects of their lives. In turn, they'll become better athletes, students, teammates, and friends.

Ultimately, it's not the head but the heart that transforms our response to fear.

A great way to implement self-compassion is to simply discuss it. During one of my Elite Performance Too-E workshops, I allowed the athletes to gain access of my mind for a moment and understand a time when I had no empathy for myself, letting them know that they're not alone.

"When I think back to my childhood," I said, "I'm flooded with thoughts before I'm flooded with memories."

Looking around at the other kids in my classroom, I remembered thinking, *Do their clothes and shoes have holes in them? Do they eat peanut butter and jelly, or mayonnaise sandwiches every day too? Do they have to boil water on their stoves for a warm bath? Do they have to steal food to eat?*

Poverty had a way of reminding me every day that I was a failure.

"My fear of failing affected so many areas of my life," I said, then shared examples of the countless times I would start something, only to give up on it the second I hit a roadblock. I graduated high school with a 1.6 GPA. I pulled myself out of the university Kevin got me into twice before I flunked out. I struggled with friends because I spent too much time trying to get them to like me, and lost myself in the process.

The young athletes looked up at me with wide eyes—eyes that, I knew, had felt the same pain at some point in their lives. My story allowed them to feel comfortable and was relatable, which eventually opened an honest dialogue about self-compassion.

Every team has its fair share of players that don't get along. It's natural, especially on teams with young players. However, this lack of compassion for teammates can severely hinder the group's performance—and I can assure you that *every* team I've worked with has this issue in one way or another. It manifests in a couple of different ways:

- Fear of judgment, which causes athletes to play it safe.

- Playing with apathy or being too cool to care, which diminishes all forms of passion.

- Bullying, which divides the team.

Regardless of the way it shows itself, this kind of behavior is harmful to the team culture and can negatively impact the season's results. It plants self-doubt, creates trust issues, and hinders communication.

Instead, learning to embrace teammates must begin with *respect*. They don't have to be best friends with each other—in fact, they don't even have to agree with each other. But they will need to respect one another in order to grow and find success. During some of my Elite Performance Too-E sessions that discuss having compassion for teammates, I circle back to the reason why I refer to teams as families. Even though families don't always get along, love for one another is present no matter what. We can duplicate this kind of environment in teams as long as we openly address the underlying issue. Pretending these tensions don't exist will only end up causing problems within the team to surface later on down the road.

\*\*\*

I knew I was in for an interesting case when I returned to consult an elite football team that had a big problem. They were typically a championship-winning program, but this year things were different. They had no experienced or groomed varsity-level quarterback.

Their next in line transferred to a different school. As a result, one of the best players on the team—a previous linebacker, running back, and field goal kicker—took on the challenge. However, there wasn't going to be any handholding or special treatment. This year would be like any other, quarterback or no quarterback.

Although this young man was a great athlete (and his eventual spot on a collegiate Division I football team proved that), he struggled at the position, which was apparent by their record. While the team had plenty of hardware to show off in the trophy case from previous seasons, going into the seventh game the team had a record of only two wins and five losses.

Thankfully, I'd worked with this team for several years, so empathy was ingrained in their culture. This became clear in the way they showed this new, struggling quarterback a tremendous amount of compassion and didn't blame him once for their shortcomings. Instead, they appreciated that he had the courage to step up and take on such a weight.

This, however, didn't change the fact that the team felt like they were letting everyone down. The school and community that had always rallied behind them in the past were suddenly quiet at games. Parents were cursing under their breath in the bleachers, and the energy at games from the students just wasn't there.

The coaching staff decided to make a bold move and bring up a talented freshman to take over the quarterback position. We did a workshop exercise where the entire team greeted the freshman with open arms by expressing their support for him. They made sure he felt accepted, included, and like he was a part of their family. In fact, the most encouraging player was the one this freshman would replace.

And because the team believed in him, he believed in himself. Miraculously, they turned around their season and won the state championship without skipping a beat. Having self-compassion as well as compassion for others is a selfless act. On the court or field, this skill elevates players and teams to new heights. This is because when experiences result in failure and disappointment, compassion expels destructive internal dialog and the fear that causes athletes to play it safe.

I always tell groups I work with that there's a gift behind being part of something bigger than oneself, and that gift is the opportunity you receive to build a collective heart. That's why, in the words of Coach Harbaugh, *nobody has it better than us.*

# CHAPTER FOUR

# UNDERSTANDING PARENTS

When I first saw my own child display athletic ability, my mind went straight to formulating an action plan that would get her to reach her full potential.

Unbeknownst to my fourth-grade daughter, my expectations of her were already quickly forming. Soon she would begin to internalize that there were measurements, results, and efforts she would have to achieve in order to appease her dad. So, when she eventually started to play basketball, I got *really* invested. I'm already a competitive person, but because I played the sport myself, I felt I had a wealth of knowledge I could bestow onto her.

I watched her skill set improve as she continued to grow. I took her to private lessons, watched hours of practices, forced her to shoot baskets on family vacations, and would go over every mistake she made in her youth YMCA league games on drives home.

Yep, I was one of *those* parents.

Speaking from firsthand experience, once an adult interjects themselves into their son's or daughter's game, the adult's perspective becomes the only one that matters. Suddenly, players inherit the parent's version of what progress looks like and what work needs to be done to achieve success.

That's why my daughter sat me down when I received the opportunity to coach her basketball team during her senior year of high school. She took my hand and said, "Dad, I'd love for you to be my coach." She stopped and held her breath. The next words were harder for her to get out. "But I just want you to be my *dad* when practice is over."

I felt a heavy weight sink into my chest. My obsession with her athletic performance had affected her in ways I was too blind to see. In becoming her pseudo-coach, I had sacrificed part of my identity as her father. It's something that still hurts my heart. That night, I made her a promise that I would separate my two roles and never again let the lines become blurred.

While this can be an extremely important and difficult realization, I understand parents because I am one. But I'm also a coach. That's why I get frustrated when I hear coaches complaining that kids today are a pain in the ass, or that you have to be a therapist and coach (these are real quotes!). I have a hard time believing there's a problem with the athletes at all, and even if these sentiments are true, we need to start considering that the issue isn't them but the culture they're raised in.

This is why in order to become better coaches, we need to understand the culture athletes are being raised in. After all, we're all just products of our environment.

# Passionate Parents

Jill was on a sixth-grade travel basketball team I helped coached. That summer, we signed up for a million different tournaments. It just so happened that at one of these tournaments there was a boys basketball travel team playing too, and many of the girls were friends with the players on the team.

Naturally, there was great excitement among the girls, who were buzzing when the boys came to watch their eight and nine a.m. games. They all discussed doing the same for the boys, who were playing at 11 a.m. at a nearby gym.

Jill's father was in the stands watching. He was dropping a ton of money on Jill's basketball endeavors, which included having her play on another travel AAU team and paying for countless private lessons. When he watched Jill perform poorly in her first two games in the tournament, naturally he was disappointed.

Around 10 a.m., everyone headed back to the hotel to get dolled up for the boys' game. It had been decided that five parents, including myself, were going to caravan them to the gym. We all met in Jill's father's hotel room and one by one the girls left to go to the boys' game. They were so excited and energetic it was incredible. You would have never known they'd just played two games.

Jill was the last one to leave. As she was approaching the door to walk out, her dad stuck his arm out across the doorway like a blockade and said, "Where do you think you're going?"

I was so taken aback that I froze.

"I'm going with my friends to watch the boys play," Jill timidly replied. She barely got the words out.

"No, you're going to stay in this room and think about your awful performance and hopefully do better in the last game today." And that's what Jill did. She sat in the bedroom and cried as all her friends left without her.

As I slowly walked out of the room, still debating whether to say something or not, I felt a deep empathy and sadness for Jill. I knew all too well what it felt like to not want to disappoint your father. But I also felt a great deal of anger towards him. Looking back at the incident now, my anger towards him was most likely a direct reflection of some of my very poor behavior I'd shown towards my own daughter.

Ultimately, the game being played wasn't just his daughter's experience, it was their joint experience—just as it was the case with my daughter and I at the time. Unfortunately, she didn't meet his expectations, and not only was he her dad but also her investor and coach.

We all know a story like this. Maybe you've been that parent, or maybe you've witnessed it happening. A parent who intensely watches every practice and every game. Constant conversations with their child about how to fix their swing on the drive home from practice or cursing under their breaths at games. The parents who call the coach on Sunday nights, or who complain to their kid about how poorly their best friend played.

It's brutal, and I don't hold any judgment about passionate parents because I was one too. However, there is a line you can cross, and it's from my own understanding and experiences why I want to help *you* understand this situation a little bit better too.

# Diagnosing the Issue

In my estimation, there are three general causes of overzealous parents: helicopter parenting, keeping up with the Joneses, and college scholarships. Let's take a look at each of these categories to get a better understanding of parental behavior as it relates to their child's athletic pursuits.

1. **Helicopter Parenting**

   Here in the United States, the general trend of parenting has swung from latchkey kids to helicopter parenting.[7] This is when a parent pays especially close attention to every single thing their child does. There's such a mass hysteria surrounding the safety that kids can no longer *just be kids.*

   But let's contemplate why. Reflect on the vast amount of change that we have experienced as a society in the past 30 years. For better or for worse, we have the power of instantaneous information at our fingertips. This often means hearing about the dangers of the world at an amplified volume—and it can often be terrifying for parents.

   I'm not sure if there's more evil in the world or if it's more publicized now, but it sure feels that way. This phenomenon is the reason why parents don't let their kids go to the playground alone anymore. There's no more walking to school alone, and no more trips to the skatepark without a parent.

   Naturally, if this is the way things are, practice becomes another concern.

It starts with thinking, *I'm just going to drop my kid off for practice and come back for the last 15 minutes in case they finish early.* Next thing you know, 15 minutes turns into 30 minutes, and 30 minutes turns into watching the whole practice. Parents get invested—and you can't blame them for it.

That's the joy athletics brings.

2. **Keeping Up with the Joneses**

Having a star athlete for a child can do wonders for a family's social standing. Unfortunately, this is the primary motivation for some parents. If their child isn't playing up to standard, it can be embarrassing to their parents. In turn, there will be more private lessons, more studying gameplay, and more shooting hoops in the driveway before dinner.

This tendency also stirs up a tremendous amount of fear for parents. The thought of little Johnny or Jane falling behind other players becomes too much to bear. Meanwhile, the parents are completely unaware that their child has nowhere near the same amount of fear they do, nor do they really care. That is, until a parent projects their fear onto their child.

3. **College & Scholarships**

Parents want their kids to succeed. Nowadays, this often requires getting into a great school. Sports are one way to do that. Scholarships can help a family save an enormous amount of money and open doors that might otherwise be shut. Unfortunately, many don't seem to recognize that the chance of their child receiving a scholarship for athletics is highly unlikely.

## Over-Coaching the Coach

Whether you're one of these parents or not, I'm sure you've at least heard the yelling in the stands, parents telling their son or daughter what to do during the game. It's likely that most parents have good intentions and honestly believe they're helping their son or daughter. In reality though, they're nothing more than a major distraction. I've found that in most cases what they're ordering their son or daughter to do is completely against what the coach wants the team to do. These parents are mainly interested in one person's success.

The problem with this is that it places the athlete in a very uncomfortable position. Do they listen to their parents, or to their coach? You tell me how a player can be laser focused and at their absolute best when they have this kind of mental distraction going on in their head. It's just not possible. Furthermore, this kind of behavior sucks the fun out of the game for the child while simultaneously embarrassing them in front of their team.

I believe *over-coaching the coach* comes down to ego and the simple fact that some parents have invested their personal time, money, and guidance into their son or daughter's journey. Naturally, they might feel that they're entitled to have a say, but this doesn't change the fact that this attitude can cause a significant amount of stress to players and prevent a team from unconditionally loving each other.

There are likely more causes, but these are the patterns I know firsthand and often see in other well-meaning parents. I also want to reiterate that most of these parents are operating from a place of love. The difficulty comes from what this type of parenting passes on to children, and how that affects their relationships with sports, their teammates, and the world.

First, let's get one thing straight. Kids want nothing more than to make their parents proud. When their parents tell them they need to work on their swing, they may scoff, but they will work on their swing. When their parents curse under their breath, they feel the disappointment they're causing. And when their parents talk negatively about another player, they'll distance themselves from them. All of this creates a culture of individualism in sports.

Lighting a fire is a useful tool that I used many times on my own daughter. It forced her to practice and practice until she had nothing left to give. But that was before Kevin.

Kevin came to help my team for the first time when I was coaching my daughter. Through my brother, I learned that this coaching methodology produced burnout and emotional drain. I also learned that my players—and my daughter—never really experienced the spirit of free play like I did when I was a boy.

We were able to expand and improve our skillset because we were not afraid to try new things, all while being unencumbered by adults judging our every move. On the walk home, we would talk about the great plays that were made during the games and laugh about the bad ones—but there was no judgement or hate sent towards those involved.

Truthfully, there was nothing like bouncing the basketballs on the way home as we talked and laughed our heads off. Knowing that my daughter and her teammates weren't experiencing this made me sad, but knowing that I was part of the problem made me feel even worse.

## A Common Struggle

When my daughter was in fourth grade, three of her friend's parents called me up and asked if I would coach their children in basketball. I hesitated with my response, as I'd decided long before that I would have nothing to do with coaching my daughter or her friends because I knew my fear would be projected onto the team. I would demand winning. I would be intense. And it would be serious business.

I felt this way because I couldn't accept failure. This struggle of mine was rooted in my relationship with my father. During childhood, the only opportunity I had to connect with him was through my success in sports. Therefore, I couldn't bear failing because that would mean I was a failure. My entire self-worth was tied to the *need* to win.

This drive for his approval didn't go away as I got older. It haunted me and would affect everything I did in relation to sports, even when coaching a grade school team. And I didn't want to put my daughter through any of that. Nonetheless, I reluctantly accepted. I did some good things, but I did some bad things too.

During the many years I coached them, I often drilled them too hard and almost always picked on the better players. When they were in eighth grade, I forced them to wear weighted vests during practice and would condition them to the point that some players would throw up. Sometimes I would fall into a rage if plays weren't being executed exactly how I wanted them to be. My face would go red, I would shake with anger, and I would yell.

I imagine seeing this would've been incredibly overwhelming for most children.

My own fear of failure seeped into my relationship with the children. If the players lost a game, it meant that I was a failure, and if I was a failure, that meant I was worthless and inadequate. As a result, I would do everything within my power to make sure losing did not occur often. The truth is no grade school basketball player should have to carry that burden.

When you peel away the onion and ask why some parents are so invested in their child's athletic career, it truly does boil down to fear. When I look back at this time, I remember thinking from the very beginning how important it was to get my daughter and her teammates signed up for tournaments that provided the highest level of competition. I didn't want this for them so they could have fun—I wanted them to win.

Today, if I ever believe a parent has internalized this same approach, I have a good inkling why. I tell them that most of their kids will be burnt out by the time they get into high school, and that when their kids have no other meaningful connection to the game except winning, they become numb to the whole experience.

Of course, there are parents who think this is all nonsense, and I get it. I felt the same way. I didn't change my mind until I coached these 12 kids on my daughter's basketball team into highly skilled players that won a ton of games in high school and noticed for myself how numb they were to the joys of the game. It became something that they did, but not something they enjoyed.

That's why I'm now devoted to making up for the damage I did. In Alcoholics Anonymous (AA), you make a list of all the people you need to make amends to. I've done that to some of those players I coached too.

In certain cases, parents have a bunch of baggage from our experiences that we throw onto our kids without even realizing it, which forces them to process fear with the same intensity as we do. In reality though, the stakes aren't that high. The goal here is to make as many parents realize this before the sport becomes too burdensome for their children to bear.

## Make a Difference

I believe there needs to be an awakening in parents. Thankfully, coaches can help them get there. Before we continue, determine whether the team can become a student's solace from home after implementing the teachings found in this book. Several athletes I've spoken to have told me they've explained to their parents how happy they are on the team even though they aren't playing that much. They feel accepted enough that they're able to stand up to their parents. If you've successfully created this space, you may not need to talk to parents. Understandably, that's not always the case. Sometimes extra measures need to be taken for a change in culture.

This is where parent workshops come in to play. Before starting, it's important to know that there will be parents who won't want to attend or believe the workshop is worthless. You might receive discouraging body language or negative comments throughout the session.

For this reason, you need to have realistic expectations. I caution you to avoid anticipating that all the parents are going to walk out of the workshop completely on board with what you're teaching. Each parent will inevitably leave your workshop feeling a different way. Some will be invested, some will be on the fence, and some may disagree with everything you've said. All these things are ok. Just keep in mind that if you can help one parent, *the effort is worth it.*

I encourage you to hold onto that hope. Avoid being confrontational with those that want to fight and instead acknowledge their truth, move on, and simply share your own observations and experiences. You want the workshop to be informative, thought provoking, and insightful—not a battle to determine who is right. At the very least, the players will usually hear the message and buy into the teachings.

With this knowledge under your belt, we're ready to get started. Get as many of the student's parents to participate as you can and begin with this step-by-step approach:

1.  Ask each parent to write down or share with the group what the most fond or joyful memories independent free play related to sports afforded them as a child. Encourage them to be specific with their examples. To better direct them, you can ask, *how many coaches were there? How many private lessons did you go to? How many parents were watching?*

2.  Next, tell them to write down or share some of the challenges they faced. *What where some of the obstacles during the game? How were problems resolved? Who resolved them?*

3.  Continue by asking the parents to write down or share with the group what they experienced with their friends while going to the playing field or court, as well as what they experienced on the way back home.

4. Then, request that they write down or share with the group what they believe the benefits of independent free play are, and how those benefits are different from what their kids experience today.

5. Finally, inquire how they think we could interject this spirit of independent free play into today's culture of organized, structured, and adult oversight to play sports.

At Elite Performance Too-E, I open this session by asking them to close their eyes.

"Imagine what it was like to play sports when we were young," I say, then go on to paint a picture of memories spent kicking a soccer ball on an unmarked field, scraping knees, and running home after it got dark. "Now that you're in that place, try to remember how many coaches were standing on the sideline, how many private lessons there were, and how many parents were around."

The difference is stark, and more likely than not, you'll see this understanding through their expressions.

"Fast forward to today," I say. "Are there any potential differences?" I ask this question with non-judgment, just as I would with any of my workshops.

Some participants respond by stating the difference, which allows me to increase the level of intervention and ask a question that points more at their own individual involvement. "What part do you personally have in adding on to your child's plate?"

Consistently, I'm flooded with responses that detail the extra coaching, the weekend drills in the backyard, the club teams, the private lessons, and the extra morning practice. When I hear this,

I remind parents again of the way sports were played in past generations. It was a place for them to have fun, bond, think, and perhaps most importantly—get a much-treasured break away from their parents.

When kids don't have this break, many of them eventually feel stress, pressure, and demands. To escape, as some of these kids grow up, they might look to drugs or alcohol, form a bad relationship with food, or turn to self-harm. While this might sound extreme, I assure you these are all things I've heard about in workshops from the kids. Sometimes, I have to share this information with the parents as gently as I can, some of whom may not even know of this behavior.

This brings me to my culminating point. Most kids today don't play sports, they *work* at them. While there are some athletes who are innately motivated by a passion to play, these players are exceptions to the rule. Others invest hours upon hours in athletics because they are forced to do it. While it's likely that they sometimes experience joyful moments, most of the time it's a burden. Contrary to the past, many players today are unable to connect to their own purpose and passion for playing because adult intervention is at an unprecedented level.

For young players, a sport isn't supposed to be a job. Athletics are supposed to be about working together, finding joy in the ups and downs, and being a part of something bigger. We've brought our individualism into something that was never meant to be individualistic. When I explain this cultural shift to parents, I'm not trying to make them feel ashamed or blame them, as it's really not their fault. They're just one person in an ever-changing civilization. After all, it's tough not to replicate the behavior seen throughout society.

With that in mind, it's important to remember that change going forward is what matters most.

# A Silver Lining

One day out of the blue during the COVID-19 pandemic, a dozen neighborhood boys appeared on the basketball court at my house. When I built this basketball court 25 years before, I envisioned a day when a bunch of kids would come and play. As it happened in front of my eyes, I thought I was in a dream, and couldn't have been happier.

Many of them came on their bikes. Some walked, and others had their parents drop them off. It warmed my heart to see these kids come from all over and from so many different walks of life. I live in a predominantly white neighborhood, but only one of the players was white.

But what I enjoyed most was that there were no parents there to comment on their child's shooting technique and no coaches to tell them what to do. And yet, as I watched them play, I noticed how they *still* competed relentlessly against each other. In between games, they laughed, joked around, and had fun just being with each other.

After about an hour and a half later, I looked out my window and saw the basketball game had turned into a football game in my backyard. They made their teams on their own, thought up funny names, and fictionalized end zones and sidelines. It reminded me of the way I used to play when I was a kid, but it also gave me hope. We have the power to bring this joy back into the game, and it's our job to make it happen.

# CHAPTER FIVE

# BELONGING

## WHAT MAKES US HUMAN

How do you keep your last-string players happy?

I'm guessing you've dealt with this problem in the past or are currently dealing with it now, because it's one of the most prevalent issues in the world of athletics. Personally, I've run into this problem on every team I've coached or work with.

Thankfully, this was another area that Kevin was able to guide me through.

Years ago, when I was coaching my daughter's basketball team, I asked him to help me after I noticed the players were emotionally muted. Wins and losses started to affect them the same way. They had lost all passion for the game, and I was worried I was the one to blame for it. I was a maniac of a coach, and was drilling them every second of every practice. They were punished for mistakes with more drills, and were taught that winning was the top and only priority. This is because to me, it was.

When I realized we were winning but not *really* winning, I reached out to Kevin for the first time. He ended up making a huge impact on everyone (including me), but there was one player in particular where his influence was particularly significant.

Colleen was the 12th player on our 12-person team. She'd participated in the basketball program since her freshman and sophomore year but decided not to come back her junior year because she wasn't going to be on varsity. She returned to the program her senior year when I became coach only because she wanted to be a part of the team.

Seven games into the season, after sitting on the bench most of the time, Colleen's mindset changed. She became apathetic, stopped hustling in practice, and lost motivation to cheer for her teammates. It was clear that she felt like if she wasn't playing, there was no point in being on the team. I could sense she wanted to quit.

Many kids feel this way when they're not getting playing time. Often, it goes back to what their parents tell them when they get home. While it's true she wasn't on the court, what Colleen didn't understand was all the other ways she was contributing to the team.

Kevin gathered everyone together for an exercise geared specifically toward Colleen. In our small pre-game room scattered with desks and a whiteboard, Kevin stood in front of the girls. They each had a piece of paper and a pencil in front of them. I'd never used the room for any other purpose than to train, strategize, or coach, so there was something special in the air that day. Kevin wore the same beaming smile he always had on when he was doing what he loved. With his hands open and welcoming, he prefaced the session by saying, "We're going to do some work with Colleen today. We need to understand how she's feeling, and if she's willing to be honest enough, we'll be able to grasp her perspective without judgment. Remember, this is her truth."

Colleen was in a chair at the front of the room, while I was standing in the corner—a fly on a wall. Kevin stepped aside for Colleen to take the stage. You could sense she was nervous, but her apprehension quickly faded when she was met by the smiling faces of her teammates. Colleen told her truth wonderfully. She expressed that she believed she brought no value to the team and was losing interest in the game because of it. She also felt like an outsider when other players talked about things they were experiencing on the court.

She captured everyone's attention and heart with her words. Many of them didn't know how she was feeling, so it affected them deeply. When she was done, Kevin requested that everyone write three things they appreciate about Colleen that had nothing to do with basketball—just what they loved about her as a person. One by one, they began to stand up and read from their list. He asked Colleen to just sit there and take every moment in. You could see the tears building up in her eyes. She was moved by what everyone was saying, but Kevin felt more could be done. He adjusted the exercise so the remaining players had to come to the front of the room and face Colleen as they spoke to connect on an even deeper level. This small modification changed everything.

Her teammates couldn't stop the tears from pouring down their face either as they talked about Colleen's kindness, silliness, willingness to help, and how she brightened everyone's day. I watched from my small corner, wiping away tears of my own. I was in awe of the simple joy of humans expressing appreciation for one another. I was also in awe of my brother.

After everyone shared their piece, Kevin stood back up and asked Colleen, "Did you know how everyone felt about you?"

She looked around the room, genuine love in her eyes for each person there. She turned back to Kevin and replied, "Coach Touhey, I had no idea." The experience had profoundly changed her. She was unaware of the hidden ways she was affecting everyone on the team. It gave her a purpose again. Before she sat back down, she told my brother that it would take the ends of the Earth to get her off the team knowing what she knew now, whether she played a second a not.

Kevin always theorized that *belonging* is one of the things we yearn for the most, but witnessing the team's acceptance of Colleen solidified that importance. Making sure everyone on your team feels like they belong is the key to keeping them fulfilled and happy, even when they're not playing. Without it, the struggle to keep team members happy and satisfied with their role will never end.

It saddens me to see how many athletic teams struggle with this problem, but as we've uncovered, it's because teams today face a cultural crisis. Individualism is foundational in our national and individual identities, and it's common to teach kids to get ahead first and be a teammate second. This leads to divisive cliques that sever a family into factions rather than building one loving unit. Instead, judgments are made about teammates, players talk behind each other's backs, and individuals put their interests first. A *not my fault* mentality is pervasive, causing every player to look to the person who threw them the ball after making a mistake.

So, how can you undo all the damage that's been done? How can you turn individualism into inclusion? Here's a hint: it doesn't start with drills.

## Searching For Belonging

While coaching a travel basketball team, I immediately noticed that two budding cliques had the potential to cause a significant distraction and challenge for the entire team. One of them consisted of Black players, while the other clique consisted of White players. The environment many of these boys grew up in were polar opposites, so judgments were being made by both groups.

I knew there was much work to be done to heal this divide, and it would start with me. It was my job to get everyone together and listen to each other with an empathetic ear. It's true that you can't always expect everyone to get along—especially in the cases where right and wrong are involved. The bigger issue in this situation for me was their unwillingness to accept one another. From my observations, their reasons were based on stubbornness, close-mindedness, and minutiae that had nothing to do with who they were as people.

Because you can't truly understand a person until you walk in their shoes, the first thing we did was give each player an opportunity to talk about what their life was like away from the school, athletic field, or court. No feedback or judgement was allowed. Our only job was to listen.

Eventually, we moved onto introducing the concept that both parties typically play a role in causing friction in a relationship, and that the notion of one person or group being at fault is a fallacy. Once both sides where open to the idea they were both contributing to the problem, we moved on to a slightly different exercise. On one side of an index card, each player wrote down the part they played in contributing to the tension. On the opposite side of the card, they wrote down the actions and steps they would take to change their destructive actions and behaviors. Finally, they gave each other permission to hold each other accountable and commit to change.

As a result of this work, each player from each clique thanked me for helping them make new friends when the travel season was over. The two groups were no longer separated by group, race, or class. Instead, they all acknowledged how their preconceptions and judgements got in the way of forming new meaningful relationships.

So, how does something like this happen? Sounds like a miracle, right?

I believe that acceptance is the fuel that allows a player to open up. It expels cliques, exposes the fear of being unpopular or unliked, eliminates prejudice and hatred, and replaces the negativity with love, understanding, and possibilities. Without the feeling of belonging, your players will be shut off emotionally, physically, and mentally from the rest of the team. Because you need every player to succeed, it's imperative that you work with your team to develop unconditional acceptance for everyone.

But creating this space starts with *you*. Coaches are human too. Some have opinions about their players' character, interests, friends, introversion/extroversion, ethnicity, sexuality, or race. Even if a coach doesn't intentionally act on their feelings, they may treat an athlete differently without realizing it by giving them less playing time or talking to them differently.

We are incredibly perceptive as humans, and your players and team as a whole will be able to sense a lack of acceptance. If you don't take care of acceptance on your end, there's no chance it will spread throughout the team.

Before continuing, I suggest you take a deep look inside and assess whether you feel this way about any of your players. If you do, and this is your first time realizing it, don't panic. This doesn't make you a terrible person. Remember that we all have unconscious biases rooted in the way we were raised based on our experiences and from society. What matters now are your actions going forward.

Self-reflection can be difficult, but it's a step that needs to happen. Each season, I recommend you take the time to look at each individual on the team and write down anything that might make you feel a little bit uncomfortable about him or her. Return to your list at the end of the season and compare the way you once felt to the way you currently feel. I'm positive there will be a difference. Not only will you grow as a person from this reflection, but you'll see the growth in your team as well.

Also, remember that you're not alone. I recently made some initial judgments about a new player based on his physique and experience in the game. He had a very thin frame, wasn't very tall, and had a low basketball IQ because he hadn't played the game for very long. I was worried he wouldn't be able to contribute physically on the court and that the entire coaching staff and players would lose patience with him.

It only took a couple of days to realize how wrong I was. He contributed so much more than I could've imagined, on and off the court. Although he was not going to help in respect to his limited basketball experience, his work ethic, positive attitude, selflessness, and love for the team was infectious. This forced me to confront why I made these assumptions so I wouldn't make others like them again.

Upon introspection, I learned that I was focused only on what this player could do for me. Once again, my own fear of failure is what caused this knee-jerk reaction. Even more disappointing was the fact that I failed to recognize how much the player was giving to the team in terms of intrinsic value. Through experiences like this one, I've learned that the first step toward acceptance is to look inside yourself. It's not always about the players. It's about *you* too.

But chances are, there are still big problems within the team that will likely need to be dealt with. These problems can present itself in the form of cliques, negativity on the sidelines, gossiping, drama, and pettiness. Obtaining the opposite of these by embracing acceptance doesn't mean your team will become one kumbaya session after another, and it also doesn't mean your team has to be the group that goes everywhere together.

Instead, acceptance is achieved when every single person on the team feels comfortable and respected enough to be themselves without having to be best friends. To get this kind of belonging, your team needs to learn about each other outside of practice. This is done by communicating who they are in relation to things that have nothing to do with the sport, including their biggest challenges, fears, hopes, and dreams.

As your team works through getting to truly know one another, players will make connections among their similarities and differences. You'll be able to look at a stereotypical jock on your team and someone who appears to be the opposite and say, "Look at how similar you guys are. Could you be more connected than you originally thought?"

Likewise, there will be stark differences among your team. In my opinion, the dissimilarities are the most beautiful because they allow you to look at two people and learn more about their realities. We all have the ability to open our minds to something new and exciting. This is why putting a focus on belonging within the team is a powerful and important venture.

Before starting this next exercise, remind everyone to listen *without* judgment. It's important to communicate that these passions are personal to the individual. We are all different, unique, and special. Negative responses should be avoided, as it will keep the player from sharing.

Here's how to get started:

Conduct a workshop session where each player writes down three interests that are unrelated to sports.

Have each student express these things to the room, explaining why they're passionate about them and how they became interested.

Finally, open the discussion up to everyone by letting the team ask questions about this athlete's interest. *How did you get into this hobby? How can I learn more about it?*

While the players share their interests, write them down on a white board. When everyone is done, take a photo of the board so you can use the interests in the future to learn more about your players.

This simple exercise allows athletes to have a better understanding of each other, create deeper friendships based on shared likes, and learn to appreciate their differences. As you move around the room, be sure to write key words on the board that are related to feelings (like happiness, joy, or curiosity). This way, you'll be able to branch emotions to one another, no matter how unique everyone's interests are.

If you can get your players to describe the feeling of doing something they love, others won't be able to tell the student they don't have the right to feel that way just because they don't get it themselves. It's critical that you make these links to allow for understanding. For example, if one person loves chess and describes it as exciting and fun, you can connect those feelings to the student who likes watching MMA for the same reasons. The person who likes MMA will suddenly be able to understand why their teammate likes chess, even if they have assumptions about chess. It doesn't mean that they will start playing, but it will expel any negativity that previously existed.

In another workshop, ask players to write down one to three things they would change about themselves if they could. Their answers are usually related to their actions, attitude, or behavior as an athlete, but they can be connected to who they are as a person, son, daughter, student, friend, sibling, and so on.

Request that they share their list and expound on why they want to change.

Ask the players that shared to describe how they see themselves in the future if nothing changes.

When a player is done sharing, ask them if they're open to receiving feedback from their teammates. Remind the team that they're not to give feedback that's advice or meant to fix anything that has been shared.

Lastly, ask the players to write out a strong statement about what action(s) they plan to take. Have the players read the statement out loud to the team. Then, ask the player if the team has permission to hold them accountable to make these changes possible.

The purpose of this exercise is to tap into vulnerability and reveal the many feelings we share as humans, no matter how different the context. Two people in entirely different situations can feel the same thing, which is a true testament to the beauty of humanity.

Remember, not everyone is going to want to share. That's ok. The important thing is that enough of the players open up, and in doing so, make an impact on those who choose not to. What they express will remind the others that they're not alone in their struggles.

Hold sessions that are dedicated to sharing any struggles or pain players are currently experiencing. Guide the team by explaining that they don't have to share anything too painful.

Once a student is done, ask the room if anyone is currently feeling a similar pain or going through a comparable struggle. Be sure to clarify that players are not to give advice or potential solutions that will fix the problem.

Then, ask the original speaker if they would like to receive any feedback or advice from their team. If they agree, inform them that some of the information will be helpful and some may not. As long as everything is coming from a place of care, that's all that matters.

Do these sessions regularly, at least once a month.

After doing these sessions, you'll be well on your way to employing the critical skill of acceptance into your program while fostering a space of belonging. These frequent workshops will prompt players to become better communicators and friends. It's also a great time to check up on your athletes and ensure they have a place to speak freely when they need to.

You might be surprised at how great of a need there is for this.

As I noted before, make sure to take photos of the board or copy what you wrote onto a notepad when a session is completed. As the coach, it's your responsibility to watch, listen, and wait for issues to bubble up. When they inevitably do, you'll be able to refer back to your list to see whether your players have grown or regressed.

Lastly, as always, don't be afraid if some of the players aren't speaking. Some kids are naturally going to want to share at a deeper level, while others won't share at all. Regardless, those who are incapable of sharing are still benefitting. They might not speak up on the day you hold your workshop, but they may at home or even years down the line.

When I talk to programs about the fact that there's something bigger going on than just the sport, they start to become more aware of the responsibility they have. Part of that responsibility is to create a sense of belonging.

Because of our individualistic culture, many people rely on their internal resources, courage, and strength to weave their way through life. But there's a problem with that, as doing so can make a person lonely, overwhelmed, and cause them to numb themselves through drugs, drinking, sex, social media, and other vices.

By creating a sense of belonging through sport, it is possible to change the direction of a person's life. Doing so instills unconditional self-worth, self-love, confidence, a strong connection between teammates, and a positive response to adversity. As a coach, the environment you build for your team can keep a player from hurting themselves, from turning to drugs, prevent disorders, and keep kids on the right path.

This may sound scary, but there's also great power in that. *You* have a purpose, and can change lives. If that isn't motivation enough, know that it will also produce wins!

## Acceptance Isn't Always Accepted

Kevin asked me to join him to speak to a high school girls basketball program that hired him to do workshops. The day we arrived, the coaches were holding team tryouts. I instantly took notice of one player. She wasn't very skilled, but I was impressed with her work ethic and tenacity. She was sprinting up and down the court, cheering every player on, and showed herself to be a very coachable player. I could also tell she was a fighter.

Even though she wasn't up to varsity standard with respect to her training, her coach placed her name on the roster with everyone else's a few days later. I too felt it deserved to be there. The coach received a call from another player the day after he put the roster out. She told the coach that several players on the team got together for a discussion, and that this particular player was gay, and it made them uncomfortable. Because of this, the group consensus was that they didn't want her there.

When I heard this, the first thing that came to mind was one of my brothers. My heart sank as I ran through memories of him trying so hard to be someone else. He was gay in a time that was even less tolerant than it is today. I always got the impression that he wanted to be interested in girls so badly, even though it was never meant to be. Back then, socializing and being in a relationship with someone of the same sex were nowhere near as open as it is today. Thank God this is a change our society has made for the better.

One of the things I learned about my brother was that it wasn't a choice to be gay. He deserved acceptance for who he was, just like this player did. I also felt that I had a responsibility to make this horrible situation better.

The next day during our workshop, I gathered everyone on the team, except for this player. The players watched me with wide eyes as I stood under the dangling basketball net. I scratched my head, not really knowing where to begin. All I could do was try my best.

"I'm not here to force my opinion on anyone," I said. "But I want to share my perspective."

I went on to share my brother's story. While listening, some of the girls kept their eyes on the ground. Others looked ashamed. "Imagine what it would be like if you had to walk in my brother's shoes for a day. Imagine that pain, the loneliness, how scary it would be to just be yourself." I added that if any of them believed it is a choice to be gay, I knew with 100% certainty that my brother was born gay—just the way God created him.

After my points had been made, I requested that they collectively take time to learn about their teammate without judgment, to be surprised by her character, her heart, and her goodness. I wanted them to see who she was beyond the only thing they saw her as and to recognize that she was an extremely special human being, just like each and every one of them.

Many of them raised their hands and expressed that they were afraid. They weren't sure how to treat her in the locker room, and weren't comfortable changing in front of her. I reaffirmed that their concerns were valid because that was *their* truth. But she had a truth too. We needed her to feel free enough to share her perspective on things.

Eventually, the team began to accept this player. The girl who initially called the coach about not wanting her on the team even reached out to say that everyone was starting to feel comfortable. They were well on their way to becoming a family. Unfortunately, that wasn't the last of it, and one night the coach received a devastating phone call.

It was the player.

She got the words out quickly, as if she had been holding on to them for a while. "Coach, I'm leaving the team."

When I heard this news, I was crushed.

The player explained that quitting the team had nothing to do with the girls. They had been kind and receptive. She said the problem was with her, and felt like she was making everyone uncomfortable, even if it wasn't true and even when the coach protested that it was *far* from the truth. She just couldn't accept it, and that by being herself she was being a burden to everyone else.

The player didn't come to practice the next day and everyone noticed. They reached out and told her she *needed* to be on the team, and that they were missing something without her.

Unfortunately, this didn't change things and they never saw her again.

Regardless of whether that player stayed with the team, they all did the right thing by creating a space where everyone could belong, which is something I'm proud of. Even though I didn't realize exactly what I was teaching back then, acceptance caused 11 players to beg for a player to come back to a team that they didn't initially want to include.

While the desired outcome wasn't necessarily achieved in the result, *belonging* changed the trajectory of the team for the better.

## Another Tough Situation

As head basketball coach during the 2020 season, a third of the way through our schedule one of my players approached me to question whether he belonged being on the team. He lacked confidence in himself, particularly about whether he had the skill or I.Q. to play the game. Even though he was one of our seniors, up until this point, he had never played on a basketball team and didn't have a lot of time on his hands to develop and grow as a player. Because of the insurmountable learning curve Kyle had to overcome to learn the fundamentals of the game, execute drills, understand team defensive rotational concepts, and run the offense, he could not help but feel that he was holding his teammates back. This was a primary reason why he questioned whether he belonged on the team.

While it's true he might not have had the experience of some of the other players, there are plenty of good reasons why I selected him to be on the team. During preseason and tryouts, Kyle was the hardest working player in the entire program. He showed tremendous dedication as a player by how much time he was spending in the gym to improve his game. Kyle was also one of our most selfless players, and constantly encouraged, supported, and pushed others to succeed. His example and presence elevated our team's work ethic and energy, and he demonstrated a passion and love for the game that was infectious. Despite these attributes, Kyle had no idea of the contributions and impact that he had on his teammates.

Since this wasn't the first time, I had to deal with a player who questioned whether they wanted to continue playing, I handled it the way I always did—the way Kevin taught me.

The next day at practice, I gathered the team together at midcourt. I then asked everyone to express what they appreciated about Kyle as a person and basketball player, because he was struggling with his position on the team. So many players raised their hand to speak. When I looked over at Kyle, I saw he was in shock. Just the number of players that raised their hands so quickly told him how much they cared about him.

One player after another talked about how selfless he was, his positivity, and how his encouragement and belief in others made them feel that they could overcome their own self-doubt. They were adamant that the family would suffer significantly if he were not a member. Kyle had no idea that his teammates felt so strongly about him. Although Kyle continued to have normal human reactions during the season about his self-doubt pertaining to where he fit in, he didn't stay in that space for long. The antidote? He absolutely loved his basketball family.

When practice was over that day, Kyle stayed behind for skill development. The rest of the team headed to the locker room, but two players turned around to work with Kyle. Even though they knew it was unlikely that Kyle would play very much, they *still* decided to stay behind for him. They easily could have decided he was not worth their time.

I believe they gave back because they were appreciative of what Kyle gave to the team. It was an expression of unconditional love. This experience with Kyle also affected the team in an unexpected way. It allowed the coaching staff, including me, to analyze the impatience we had with Kyle from time to time—which was almost to the point of wondering whether he should be on the team or not. I am certain that Kyle sensed it. This was a kid that gave everything, yet in return, the coaching staff isolated him. Fortunately, the exercise ended up being a huge lesson for the coaching staff, and was a wake-up call that showed us the ways we could improve too.

This is one of the blessings in doing this kind of work. If coaches are willing to be humble and open to learning, players can help coaches grow just as much. What happened with Kyle made me think about the importance of players feeling comfortable enough to approach and talk with a coach about anything. When a program invests time to develop and foster an environment grounded in acceptance and belonging, the depth and meaning behind the honest communication that occurs can be life changing.

For example, my travel team's locker room was divided by race. The Black players stuck to the left, and the White players stuck to the right. This is the same team that had several players quit a year earlier because they hated each other, and were generally players filled with rage, hatred, and ignorance.

While we were able to flip this attitude and feelings around, this kind of change requires work. You'll have to consistently do the exercises and dig deeper internally so you can become a model of acceptance for others. And it requires fostering a culture within your program where everyone feels encouraged to be themselves. Sometimes it won't go to plan, though. There will be players who are unwilling to change. In those instances, developing the culture you desire may require you to put in extra effort with an athlete or, in more severe cases, let go of them—especially if their destructive attitudes or behaviors are affecting the team.

It's easy to understand why we don't always take time to do these types of exercises. For one, they're hard. There's great difficulty that comes in getting people to change, to share their feelings, and be emotional—but that doesn't mean the effort should be avoided. Belonging, through acceptance, is the only way to counteract the individualistic mentality pervasive in athletics today. Not only will a team's performance soar, but each player will also feel like they have a purpose. They will recognize they have value beyond just what they can do for their parents, a coach, or a team.

As a result of this, your team will reach an elevated level of playing that shows their fight and spirit after every whistle. That kind of heart doesn't come from practicing a thousand shots or doing a hundred more drills—it comes from being a part of a family.

Kevin always said we longed for belonging, but I had to learn why.

We need it because it's *beautiful*.

# CHAPTER SIX

# EMPATHY

## SLIP INTO SOMEONE ELSE'S SNEAKERS

I was asked to attend a meeting with David, a college player I'd been working with, to discuss something serious. Before he spoke, I noticed his body language—how he sat across from me with his hands resting in his lap, and the way his face drooped sullenly.

We were in that office because he'd been very disrespectful to a professor, a slip-up that quickly made its way back to me. What made the situation even more dubious was that the issue that caused the snap reaction seemed trivial. David was already facing consequences for his actions from the university, but I made an effort to talk to him because I knew David's aspirations to be a leader. Sure, he was a talented player, but being a leader was more than that, and was a goal he'd expressed to me many times.

During the meeting, I was honest with him and his coach about the work we'd done together. I explained my leadership philosophy and the routes David might take going forward. In my estimation, we could handle this a few different ways. David's coach could discipline him for doing something he knew was wrong and threaten to take away any leadership role he had. This scare tactic, along with the shame and guilt he was feeling, would probably be effective for a short time until he ultimately did it again. "But that doesn't help you in the long run, now does it?" I added. David nodded his head in agreement.

"Instead," I offered, "we could talk about it. Let's see if you're willing to get at the root of the anger that you direct towards others. But, for that to happen, you need to be open and honest. Are you willing to do that?"

Again, David nodded his head in silence.

"Good," I said. "David, do you think you can be a strong leader on this team if you have that kind of rage? Do you think it's ok for a leader to demonstrate anger like that?"

"No, not at all," he earnestly replied, then dropped his shoulders in defeat. "I'm trying really hard, but I can't help myself."

"I know. David, I've seen such a great change in how you react to situations that might have caused you to be rageful in the past. So, I want to be clear that I recognize some of your progress. But I still want to know why you're so angry."

"Well, my teacher made me—"

"No, that's not what I'm asking," I said, cutting him off. "Why are you so angry?"

"What do you mean, Coach Touhey?"

"Why is there this pent-up anger in you that can explode at any minute? The things you're experiencing don't line up with the response you give back. A teacher telling you to get off the internet and do your work in class doesn't match the rage you threw at him. Why do you feel the need to do that?"

His eyes, which had been alert and on guard up to that point, fell to look at his twiddling fingers. He swallowed, and I could tell his words would be harder to get out. "Coach Touhey, I don't trust many people because I'm a Black man and I always have to be on guard. I'm angry because I have to worry about what might happen to me just because I'm Black. I'm angry because I can't just go for a walk. I'm angry because I have to worry about what will happen to my family. I have so much rage inside of me because I have to deal with this. You and my teacher are both White—you have no idea."

I felt the pain in his voice and was devastated. At the same time, I was so incredibly proud of David for having the courage to open up. I hesitated for the next few moments and questioned what to say next. How could anything I say have any meaning, compared to what the person across from me just shared? I slowed down, found the words, and regained confidence. I reminded myself that empathy is humanity's superpower.

"David, I can't even begin to imagine what that feels like. Even though I will never be able to fully understand what you go through on a daily basis, I do know what rage feels like. I've felt it towards my father, and at my situation when I was younger. It's not fun. Please know that I have so much empathy for what you're experiencing and how you're feeling.

"I will never ask you not to feel what you feel, nor will I judge that kind of anger, but we can work on no longer internalizing that life isn't fair and allowing that attitude to dictate your self-destructive actions.

"What if you said instead, 'Life is unfair and it sucks, but I'm going to respond in a way that is going to change it?' Barack Obama feels the same injustice as you. But instead of using it as a scapegoat for failure, he used it as motivation to change the world. Martin Luther King Jr. did the same thing. Doc Rivers, one of the most successful coaches in the NBA, once said, 'We keep loving this country and this country doesn't love us back,' and yet he continues to push on, live to be the solution, and inspire others.

"It's true that you have restrictions just because you have melanin in your skin. There's no denying it, and I hate that it's true. But you can take this situation and use it as fuel for leadership. You can take a challenge and respond in a way that amplifies you and your excellence. Be a person that makes a difference. And know that there are some people who can be trusted, even someone who looks like me."

## Humanity's Superpower

Whenever I ask my team what the word *empathy* means, many of them have no idea, or why it's so important that we develop it in our programs.

Culturally, empathy is a strong counter to individualism. Feeling what another person is going through and being able to understand their circumstance is a critical skill that ultimately connects people to each other on a deeper level. Furthermore, the byproduct of empathy will be teammates that play with heart and passion for each other and who carry this valuable skill with them for the rest of their lives.

So, if empathy is so treasured, why is it so hard to open up?

Frankly, the level of trust and intimacy required to do those things is tough for everyone, and kids have an especially hard time doing so because of they don't want to be judged. It's scary to share something personal without any clue of how others are going to react. This is especially understandable if past reactions have been less than positive.

To be clear, I don't want to discount all the good today's generation is doing. Like I said before, I'm forever grateful that people are much more accepting today. But I also think that social media is a double-edged sword that can make a teenager's experiences more difficult. I can't imagine what it must feel like to grow up seeing other people's perfect, though often largely fictionalized, lives on the internet every day, forcing you to hold a magnifying glass to your own faults. For me, empathy would be even more difficult to express if I was feeling incredibly self-conscious.

During a workshop, a boy named Joe decided to share something deeply intimate. He talked about his struggles with school, how he thinks he's not as smart as everyone else on the team, and that there are times when he feels incapable of doing the work.

Guess how his teammates responded?

With laughter and jokes. That was their way of coping with the discomfort they felt from going to a place they usually don't go to with others, particularly other men. Heck, even Joe laughed along with them, even though his body language told a different story. He looked absolutely defeated.

Watching Joe accept failure as part of his identity in that moment was hard to watch. I empathized with him because I did the same thing. I had a 1.6 GPA in high school, not because I was stupid, but because I didn't care about my academics. There eventually came a time when I felt dumb because that was what everyone said I was. Even though I was devastated every time someone made fun of me and my grades, I laughed along with them—just like Joe.

Because I understood Joe's situation deeply, I decided to share with the room that I dealt with the same exact thing in high school. "Joe," I said. "You aren't stupid. In fact, you're very smart and can achieve whatever you put your mind to doing."

The next thing I did was turn to the room, hoping to highlight a teachable moment. "Why did we make a joke about Joe when he opened up?" I asked. "He trusted you enough to share his feelings and look at how you reacted."

At the core of these sensitive feelings is embarrassment and an inability to see how these things are related to basketball. There are going to be a lot of kids that don't want to share their feelings because it'll be too intimate or anti-*macho*. That's why when you integrate empathy, you need to get down to the basics of what it is. Start with the definition. *Empathy is the ability to understand and share the feelings of another, because you have experienced the same feelings.* If some individuals still have a tough time understanding, include a few personal experiences to make it more relatable. Once they comprehend what empathy is, try to explain the benefits. This will make it easier to grasp its importance.

Here are a few key points I like to relate during my workshops:

1. **It's important to develop a deeper connection of intimacy.** The more intimate the team is with each other, the more powerful it will be. A better connection among players translates to more passion, more fight, and more resiliency on and off the court.

2. **Provide hope to those in need.** Empathy gives one the ability to be in another's darkest place and help them out of it. By being empathetic, your players can give someone struggling the hope they need to overcome tough obstacles they might be facing.

3. **It will make the world a better place.** When you're empathetic, your kindness spreads and causes others to do the same.

You may be thinking, *This sounds great, Patrick, but how is it going to help us win? Why are we bringing this into a sport?* I get a lot of doubts about whether empathy and other similarly intense emotions, belong in athletics. The truth is they belong now more than ever because of how shallow sports has become. Today, the primary focus of athletics is on power, successes, and outcomes. Wins, individual statistics, championships, and scholarships are what people have come to value instead of all the benefits that can be gained from being part of a team.

And the only way to recover what we've lost is to do the opposite of what we've been doing.

## Empathy Is Unbeatable

When an intentional commitment is made by a coaching staff to engrain and execute empathy into a program, it signals to players that we care for them as people. This creates an environment that offers opportunities for players to open up about their darkest fears and their most painful struggles in order to recognize that we all feel flawed in one way or another.

This is why coaches have such a tremendous responsibility, as there's an opportunity to truly impact a player's life. Unfortunately, sometimes a coach doesn't realize this until it's too late.

At a school I do workshops for, I heard about a player I was not working with that was going through a tough time. Most couldn't tell, as he was always smiling. He'd never told anyone about his depression, and was the epitome of what most people who consider to be a perfect student.

His suicide was a shock, and the fallout was immense. Parents, students, and teachers grieved, wondering what they could have done differently to help him. You'd be shocked to hear how many players display suicidal ideation in sessions. Whenever I hear that, it gives me pause, and often I step back and say to myself, *You're damn right this is important.* It makes me feel blessed to be able to do the work I do through Elite Performance Too-E, particularly because of my own experience with contemplating suicide. I know what it feels like to be in anguish, despair, and pain, and to feel like you're stuck in a dark hole all alone.

That's why it's so important that if you ever hear a player express suicidal ideation, make sure you reach out to the proper resources, such as the athletic director or an on-campus counselor. My perspective is such that lives can be saved when we setup an environment that allows for people in this kind of pain to open up without fear of being judged. But we must talk about it. Teen suicide rates have steadily climbed in the social media age. In 2015, the suicide rate among teenage girls hit a 40-year high, while teenage boys' suicide rate per 100,000 went from 10.8% to 14.2% in just five years. [8]One study found that more social media use correlated with worse self-reported physical health, mental health, and well-being.[9]

We have to educate, empower others, and let people know that if they're courageous enough to share their story, it will help others who feel the same way. I truly believe addressing and talking about suicide should be part of every athletic program, especially at the high school and collegiate level. The more we can normalize this very sensitive topic, the more people will reach out before it is too late.

Remember, players today have so much more to deal with than prior generations. There's pressure in school, judgement from peers, social media, politics, and a dying planet to worry about. The sense of community that we used to have and the idea of being a part of something bigger than yourself is different now. The good news is empathy can change that.

Because empathetic listening requires both parties to be totally present and set aside any ego, ulterior motives, or self-interest, it allows two people to connect on a deeper level. Nothing else becomes more important than listening to another human's experience. Think of empathy as a vessel that can be filled with trust, love, concern, care, protection, and acceptance. I felt these qualities were abundant when community meant sitting out on the front porch and talking with my friends, going to the local high school athletic games to give support, attending church on Sundays, or even something as simple as community picnics or playing in the street with all the neighborhood kids.

Empathy has the ability to give us some sense of that same experience.

## Brotherhood

Whenever I think about empathy, I think about my brother.

I embarrassed him twice at the university where he was a head coach. He gave me two opportunities to play there, and I disappointed him each time because of my excessive drinking.

After the second failure, I moved back into my parent's home but found the dysfunctional environment there was no easier. Instead of sticking it out, I moved in with an old high school friend, one who would enable my bad habits. My drinking got worse and I started to feel like I was dying on the inside.

Even though I was spiraling, Kevin never gave up. He talked to our parents frequently and always asked about me. Just after I left my parent's house, Kevin called our mom. She told him that I was in bad shape and was living with someone they knew would be a bad influence on me. This is when I received an unexpected call from Kevin. He asked me to come to a family gathering at our childhood home while he was home on vacation. Despite my hesitance, I showed up just to see him.

I arrived having already drunk several beers. After an hour of fake smiling and suppressing how I was really feeling, Kevin pulled me outside and said, "I'm concerned about you. How are you doing?" For the first time in a long time, I let my wall down and told him that I was very lonely and felt like I was heading down a path that didn't have a good ending. I couldn't hold back my tears.

What I appreciated most was that he didn't say that I was a loser, point out how messed up I was, or explain how I needed to get my act together. He didn't judge me at all. Instead, he showed me an immense amount of empathy and love, inviting me back to the university so I could get my degree and be an assistant coach on his staff. I knew deep down in my soul that if I didn't take my brother up on his offer, things would've ended up badly for me. In a way, I can say my brother truly saved my life.

When I'm coaching a team or workshopping with them, I often hear them shout the word *brotherhood* or *sisterhood*. But what I see is the opposite. I've watched a player open up to their teammates about their depression while their brotherhood coil in discomfort. I've witnessed judgment when people talk about their deepest fears and insecurities. I've seen teammates disappear when their sister needed them most.

Is that what a brotherhood or sisterhood is? When you describe to your team that your program is going to go deeper than simply using the words brother or sisterhood, they'll understandably resist. This can be a tough place to start as a coach.

Making these changes is going to force you to get to know your players on a deeper level than what's been required of you previously. It will entail that you share things you never imagined you would in the hopes that it'll make your team comfortable enough to do the same. Afterall, the best stories in the world are of those who went above and beyond what their job required, right? It may not be what you thought you signed up for, but it's what you need to do.

# A Venue for Change

When Elite Performance Too-E started to work with the coach of a highly competitive, successful D1 athletic team about two years ago, he pulled me aside and said, "I'm telling you this now, and I'll continue to tell you this time and time again. Winning has to occur first and foremost before we can even begin to think about fixing our culture."

I didn't react strongly because I understood where he was coming from. Eighty percent of my mindset back in the day was focused on what I could do to win. If I had skilled players acting out, I would ignore their bad behavior and think, *They'll score seven points for me on Tuesday. That'll make up for this.*

Recently, I had a one-on-one with the same coach. After a 30-year career and compiling hundreds of wins, he told me, "Patrick, you've had an impact on me, and I'm so embarrassed about the way I acted and thought before. I want you to know that building a culture around core values and excellent character is going to be our primary focus. I'm buying in."

See that?

Making these changes and winning aren't mutually exclusive. If your team has the skill, the byproduct will be winning, and in some cases even if your team doesn't have the skill, winning is still possible. We have to stop letting our fear of losing hold us back from being open to new possibilities.

So, instead of saying empathy doesn't belong on the court or field, ask yourself, *Why doesn't it?* I was a young kid that struggled in many ways, but being around leaders and mentors that had empathy for me saved my life. I'm truly not sure I would be here today if not for them. How many kids out there are like me? How many aren't getting empathy? Make your court or field the place where they can receive it. All it entails is awareness. As you go forward, there will be plenty of opportunities to be empathetic if you pay attention.

Most of the time, people look the other way because it's easier to do nothing. But it's not what's best for the world. The bigger picture is that you've been given a venue for change and you shouldn't squander it. Instead, be grateful that every morning you have an opportunity to make a real difference.

# CHAPTER SEVEN

# THE INTEGRITY ASSISTANT
## CREATING THE DRIVEN INNER PLAYER-COACH

It all started with a player I did individual sessions with named Jill, who you met in chapter four. She was still a senior but was being forced to play like she was in a D1 collegiate program, and had already decided she didn't want to play basketball after high school.

The year I started individual sessions with Jill was the year everything changed for the better. All I did for the *entire* year was give her opportunities to express how she felt and the weight she carried from playing the game. Years and years of drills, workouts, private lessons, and tournaments had taken their toll. The fire she once had for the game had gone out. The changes the coach made to the program made Jill a lot happier, but they coincided with a new game plan. Jill accepted this and adjusted her focus to helping her teammates succeed. She shared the ball more, encouraged her friends to shoot more shots, and helped the team overall become less one-dimensional.

My individual sessions helped pull her out of misery and into a space where she was able to discover herself and finally have fun. That led her to do some soul searching, and the conclusion she came to was that she didn't love basketball the way she once did but was scared to admit it because of her father. When she approached him about how she felt, I can only speculate that he reacted with anger and attributed her true feelings to my influence. I became the scapegoat.

Within a couple hours, he was sitting in the principal's office, filing a formal complaint alleging I somehow brainwashed Jill to end her career. He complained about the individual sessions I held with players, and how I was going to ruin the lives of every kid on the team if the principal didn't do something about it. Although the principal was left with a picture of me that was full of lies, he was forced to start an investigation.

Full of panic, I picked up the phone. The ringing seemed to get louder and louder, piercing my ears. Then, after a moment of silence a voice broke through.

"Hello?"

"Kevin, thank God." I sighed, but the weight in my chest didn't go away like I'd hoped. "They're going to fire me as life coach. I don't know what to do."

Like always, Kevin knew what to say. "Patrick, I know for a fact that all the work you do comes from a place of love and care for the players. You want them to have fun and feel passion for the game, right? If that's true, you need to let go of the outcome. Stay true to your integrity."

After our call, I found myself feeling at peace with what might happen. There was no shame in my time with each of the players because I had done the best I could, and that was what mattered. As it turned out, within a week or two into the investigation Jill solved these problems on her own. She went straight into the principal's office and told him that everything her dad had said was untrue. It must've taken a lot of courage for her to go against him like that—but that's just how it goes with integrity.

## What We're Missing

Think about your team. Is there room for improvement when it comes to integrity? If your experience is anything like mine is, the answer to that question is probably yes.

Whenever I inspect why that is, I always come up with the same thought: *leeway*. The rope we've extended in regard to integrity has become much too long. We've become so lost in this regard, and there are too many societal norms that shouldn't be as widely accepted.

Where can we see this? Look at how your team responds to a drill. Do they half-ass it? How many of them touch the line when running ladders? How many reps do they do when they're given a set-amount? How many blow off the details in drills? How many slack off whenever coach isn't looking?

I believe that integrity is compromised on most courts, fields, and areas outside the sport. It's alarming to me because I've always looked at sports as being a place to form future leaders. It just naturally happens in athletics—a player might find themselves in a position to lead, inspire, or coach other players. Although I still believe that leaders are made in athletics, I now find that it's not a primary focus, so it doesn't happen as frequently as it used to.

## Where Has Integrity Gone?

When I first tried to pinpoint the problem with integrity, I theorized what might have caused it. One of my guesses was that my team was a product of their environment. The road to success sounded long and daunting, so to get there they would avoid struggles and take shortcuts. That hypothesis seemed to hold when I looked at the world at large and the way we've taught our youth.

Social media values materialism and surface-level interactions. This isn't to mention that for the past four years, in the prime of their adolescence, teens saw a President on TV and Twitter with no integrity. This is a man who tweeted, "If Hillary Clinton can't satisfy her husband, what makes her think she can satisfy America?" And of course, the infamous, "Grab 'em by the—" comment. You can fill in the rest.

How do you think young, impressionable people are affected when they see a man like this in the highest form of power behave this way? I believe it teaches them that integrity doesn't matter, and that it's possible to get even farther *without it*. While I still believe all these factors contribute to the issue, an epiphany on integrity came to me.

I turned on the TV one weekend to watch the Northwestern University football team play against Wisconsin. It was a great game, but the thing that shocked me more than the surprise plays, strategies, and catches was a little wooden sign. At the end of the game, the Northwestern players headed for the locker room, where one player was holding up the purple plaque in the end zone area. Every player was enthusiastically jumping up and touching it.

When the camera finally zoomed in close enough, I saw what it said. *Trust yourself.*

It's common knowledge that trust is a significant block in most people's way, especially young athletes. The trust we're talking about in sports is not related to players trusting their coaches and authority figures (although that can also be a very real problem as well), but rather that they don't trust themselves.

You see, if trust was present, they would have no problem completing every drill correctly, no matter who was watching. If they trusted themselves, they would do every rep requested because anything less would promote feelings of guilt. If they trusted themselves, they wouldn't feel the need to cheat, and would know they could accomplish whatever they put their minds to. Northwestern's sign told me that the head coach understands the real challenge as it pertains to integrity comes from within.

## It Starts at the Beginning

If you want to do anything about this problem, you'll have to go back to the beginning for a *full reset*. Start by taking a firm stand on accountability and integrity by educating your team on those topics. Although I'm sure your team knows the definition of integrity, you can no longer take for granted that its meaning is common knowledge.

While this might not seem that necessary, you really do need to begin with the basics, because when you look around, you'll see more people in power being rewarded for a lack of integrity.

Self-serving politicians, corporations that put money before the health of people and the planet, and the fact that one in five women experience some form of rape during their lifetimes is only the tip of the iceberg.[10]

While this might seem absurd, there was a time six athletes at a university I worked with chased female students early in the morning, pretending they were going to sexually abuse them. It was a game they made up. When reprimanded, their parents defended them, saying they were "just being boys," and that they "should be forgiven."

Thankfully, the university took a firm stance on this and expelled them, but it shouldn't have happened in the first place. In my mind, this kind of behavior takes place for one of two reasons. Either integrity isn't being taught because we think it's such basic knowledge, or we're saying that winning and success is more important, and that we should all look the other way.

You may be thinking I'm being dramatic or that there are examples of people who are the exact opposite of that, but I would just say you need to take a deeper look at your team as well as yourself. In what ways are you looking the other way?

There comes a point where even though a kid will help your team win a ton of games, you have to draw the line and say enough is enough, because guess what? That's doing them a favor. What I'm challenging you to do right now is to hold yourself accountable and have as many sessions as needed to discuss and teach integrity.

# The Definition

Begin with a definition. Sit down with your players and introduce the word integrity and see how people on the team define it. In my experience, a common answer is, integrity is how you perform or act when no one's watching. While this isn't entirely untrue, it also needs to be pointed out that you're not just talking about athletics. Integrity is about every part of you, including your actions, words, and gestures. What does integrity mean to them in those spaces?

Ask them to write it down on a piece of paper. Writing it out provides a visual and allows each person to reach a higher degree of connection with the heart. Afterwards, highlight the consequences that can occur when a person doesn't act with integrity, and highlight the benefits that can occur when a person does act with integrity. Just like the other exercises, put these lists up on a board and draw commonalities or distinctions between them.

Next, pinpoint the areas in your team's life where integrity is needed. Maybe trash is being left in the locker room, or the gym floors need to be cleaned before practice, or there's a need to end gossip about other players. Take a vote and circle the top area. That's what your team will work on first.

To review, these are the steps you need to take to implement integrity:

1.  Introduce the word *Integrity* and ask for its definition. Make sure your group isn't just referencing to integrity in athletics, but in the world. Have them write their answers down on a piece of paper.

2. Highlight the consequences of not acting with integrity by asking the players what they are. Create a list on the whiteboard based on their responses. Some examples are phrases like, *less meaningful connections* and *people won't be able to trust you.*

3. Highlight the benefits that integrity brings. Create a list.

4. Have a team discussion about the areas where they think they lack integrity. Create a list based on the team's input.

5. Going off the list you just created, form a plan of action that outlines how the team will work on integrity in these areas. Make sure there is also discussion about how accountability will be executed. Maybe it's picking up after themselves in the gym and locker room, or dedicating five post-practice minutes to clean up. Whatever it is, they need to figure out the solutions themselves.

Finally, in another exercise, ask these questions:

1. "What do you not trust about yourself?" Have each player write down what they identify.

2. Next, have each player share how their lack of trust in themselves gets in the way of their integrity. Take suggestions from each player and the team regarding how they will hold themselves accountable.

If you're still asking yourself why it's important for a team to dedicate this much attention to integrity, what you'll receive in return, or what might happen if the investment in integrity isn't made, the answer is simple. Without it, your players will never reach their highest potential and they'll never trust themselves or each other without reservation. They will cheat or make a million excuses to justify why their actions outside the scope of integrity were acceptable.

On the other hand, building integrity within your team is incredibly rewarding. The most obvious and immediate benefit will be a strengthening of trust. You may also see more leaders develop, and you're likely to see overall performance improve as players learn that they can lean on each other. Beyond all of this, integrity is important even if it's for nothing more than the sake of morality. It doesn't just matter that someone is winning, it matters how they're doing it too.

## Purpose

On paper, my players and I had something in common. The first time I walked into the gym, many of the Black players could not make eye contact with me. They had absolutely no trust in me whatsoever. I imagined some of the thoughts that went through their heads: *What can this White guy possibly have in common with me?* I had a family that was stable and happy. I founded a multi-million-dollar company. I owned a big house on the opposite side of town. I mean, I seemed to have the perfect life. You could run down the list and find very little in common between us.

What they didn't know was that my life hadn't been as perfect as it seemed, and I didn't shy away from sharing this with the team. During my Elite Performance Too-E workshops, I was as vulnerable as possible and told them about the poor choices I made, the hardships I'd gone through, and the childhood trauma that still affects me to this day.

Slowly but surely, the players let down their guards as I continued to share my own flaws. I made this conclusion because of how their eyes met mine in every single workshop we did, which was a huge transformation from the boys who wouldn't make eye contact with me at the beginning of the year. Their entire presence began to hold onto just about every word I spoke. This was yet another affirmation for me that vulnerability builds trust.

One day, I even received a text from one of my players asking if there was anything he could do for me because he was trying to make a buck on the side. I responded that I needed someone to rake the leaves in my yard but warned him that I'm as detail-oriented with my lawn as I am as a coach. He joked, *Are you going to make me run sprints?* Luckily for him, that wouldn't be the case!

I was interested to see how he would do the first time he came. Would he do a half-ass job, yet still want to be paid what I promised? Would he take short cuts? Would he find an excuse not to complete the job? Up to this point, this specific player and I had done a lot of work on integrity, and I was hopeful that it would be reflected in his work. For that reason, I shouldn't have been surprised at the state of my lawn after he left, but I couldn't help but smile. You could have eaten your dinner off that lawn!

In that moment, something came over me. Looking at the work he'd done showed me how far this player and I had come together. I knew he didn't want to let me down, even when it came to my backyard, because he knows I care about him in a way that has nothing to do with basketball. Although our relationship evolved over time, the degree in which he completed the task with integrity had more to do with his development—particularly his self-worth, self-love, and self-trust. These three necessary attributes dictated his actions to be in line with conducting himself with integrity.

As a coach, I have to ask myself all the time, *What's your purpose?* For me, the answer is simple. My purpose is to help develop young ladies and men into the absolute best possible version of themselves. If that's your goal as well, you'll know that doing so requires more than just hoping it occurs through osmosis. It requires a lot of hard work. You'll have to go deeper, beyond drills, statistics, and form. But the beautiful thing about athletics is that it's meant to go deeper. It's meant to be about the ups and downs, the relationships formed, and the joy of the game.

And if you want a perfectly clean lawn while you're at it, then what are you waiting for?

CHAPTER EIGHT

# YOUR FUTURE LEADERS AREN'T BORN, THEY'RE MADE

"How would you define leadership?" After throwing this question out to my team, I got a myriad of responses. The general consensus was that a leader should have attributes like trustworthiness, loyalty, honesty, and courage. They could easily regurgitate what they'd seen from leaders in movies, on television, and in comics. While those noble concepts still hold some truth and importance, the answer I was looking for was much simpler.

My feeling is that *leadership is the ability to influence and motivate others*. In my eyes, this is a modest but accurate description. So, if it's that easy, why do so many kids find endless obstacles in their path when seeking to become a leader? Why is there such inconsistency with strong leadership year after year?

I believe it has everything to do with self-worth and not wanting to hurt their teammates' feelings. Potential leaders, like everyone else, are scared of not belonging, not being liked, being ostracized, and being alone. It all boils down to wanting to be accepted—I mean, who doesn't want to be? It's a completely normal feeling, but it's much more prevalent in teenagers. As a result, if a player's self-worth is lacking, becoming a leader will be a big challenge. Their leadership style will be centered on approval, inside-the-box thinking, and not wanting to step on anyone else's toes. Do not be fooled by the player who on the outside appears to be full of confidence and self-worth. Sometimes it's this player that lacks these qualities most.

Being a leader means you have to be ok with sometimes living on an island by yourself. To do that, a strong sense of self is necessary, and you'll need to be confident in yourself and your abilities without being arrogant. As you can see, leading is complicated, which is why we have a real problem developing leaders.

I find leadership to be a common challenge among the teams I work with. Sometimes you'll get a young man or woman who innately has leadership skills. What is more common is to find teams where true leadership is severely lacking. On the other hand, one of the best things about athletics is how it can build future leaders—and in many ways, sports were intended to do just that.

I worry that values under the umbrella of leadership like care, selflessness, and love for others are too often replaced with new, lesser ones, such as production, skill, perfection, profits, and margins. That's why the game can feel so shallow at times, and why the number of leaders has significantly decreased over time. Passionate and purposeful leadership comes from intrinsic connections to others. Extrinsic fuel such as production, winning, and profits present a roller-coaster of emotions, which have the potential to drain leadership abilities and cause feelings of drudgery.

## Let Leadership Grow

In my Elite Performance Too-E workshops, I often hear coaches say, "I'm not sure this team could ever have a leader that points us in the right direction." You may have thought or said this before as well, and that's ok if you have.

What I want to know is, how are *you* going to change that? Because it may seem like we have no control over who becomes leaders on our teams, but we absolutely do. Leaders aren't born, they're made. And if you don't take the initiative to make them, your chances of dealing with drama, division, and negativity will grow exponentially.

Changing the state of leadership on your team is a process like anything else. It also requires that you accept the difficult truth that for some players the obstacles in route to becoming a leader may be too big to overcome. For those who are up to the challenge, developing leadership requires you to ask your team an important question: "Why do you have such a strong desire to be liked, to not rock the boat, or have conflict?

The most common answer I receive is that they don't want to risk being isolated or ostracized from their teammates. Another is that they believe their teammates are unlikely to change anyway, so the risk is not worth it. After hearing the player's answers, follow up with another question that pertains to leadership. "How many times have you been in a situation where you followed through with something you know is wrong, goes against your core values, or that could be destructive to the team, just so you could fit in?"

When I ask this question, almost everyone raises their hands. Why do people sell themselves out like this? That's not true belonging.

Wanting acceptance is human nature, but receiving it at the cost of forfeiting who you are is dysfunctional. In most cases, there's something else they're starving for. I believe for many it comes down to the fact that they don't like some things about themselves. The only way many people feel they can be accepted, and therefore loved, is to conform. In essence, they're seeking acceptance for a version of themselves that isn't real.

This signifies the need to change themselves in order to get love because they can't be loved in their most authentic form. It all boils down to this: *I'm only of value when I deliver successes and accolades because that's what I've been taught to do. My self-worth is on a roller-coaster ride based on outside circumstances, whether they be athletic, academic, or socially related.*

Can you imagine the pressure of leading with that? Having to constantly put up a façade of having it all together while you're secretly dealing with these obstacles and demons inside? In my opinion, it would be impossible to keep from getting even further removed from your authentic self.

Once your players come to a point where they realize it's about them and their lack of self-worth, the goal is to help them understand why they feel that way. Have a conversation and ask them why they might feel unlovable. I know it's a stark question, but it's one that's necessary. Their answers might surprise you too, especially since perfectionism tends to be a common theme among them.

Many assume leading equates to making commands and expecting others to follow. Therefore, if someone challenges them on an order and in essence claims that the leader might be wrong, they get sensitive and fight back. Why? Because if a leader is wrong, they must be a failure. The logic to this is, *I have failed, and failing is unacceptable. I must be perfect.* The hairs on the back of their neck stand up and they go into fight or flight. And leaders always fight, right?

Wrong. They influence and motivate. That's it. Good leaders need to remain open to other people's input, listen to it, and not take it as a personal attack. They need to determine if there's a better way to do things, admit it, and adapt. They need to have enough humility to say, "You're right. That's better."

Whenever a player expresses that they want to be a leader, I tell them this: "Your sole responsibility as a leader will be to get to know the players well enough so you know how to influence and motivate each and every one of them. What works for one may not work for another. This will require you being open enough to listen, learn, and let go of your ego. Can you do that?"

Now, when it comes to finding the players that can be leaders, pay attention to the way players answer the questions above. Some of them won't be able to look inside and find the answers yet, and that's ok. But there will also be ones that are able to do just that, on top of expressing it to the rest of the team. Those are your potential leaders.

All in all, I'm not saying that finding leaders, developing them, and making them great is easy to do. I get that. But changing the way we teach leaders will make a huge difference in your program and the lives of your players. Taking these steps may feel unfamiliar, too deep, and much larger than anything you know how to do as a coach. Heck, it might even feel uncomfortable. Still, I urge you to remember that it's necessary because the lack of self-worth present today is almost an epidemic. Your players will never grow as athletes, leaders, and people until it's addressed.

## Developing Leadership Over Time

The initial work of having a player identify and work through what's blocking them from becoming a strong leader is just the beginning. Following up with your leaders will be necessary, and I would suggest you do so at least every two weeks in a meeting. During these meetings, you should use the following as a guideline for the discussion with these leaders. Be conscious to not give them solutions, directions, or answers so that you aren't controlling the meeting:

1. "How do you think things are going overall?"

2. "Do you feel that you are still struggling with some of your personal blocks?" If the answer is no, yet you continue to observe that they're struggling, bring that out into the open for discussion.

3. "Are you struggling in any way to influence, mentor change, or provide corrections to the team?"

4. "Is there anything you've identified or discovered from leading the team that you didn't expect to see?

5. "Are there any urgent or critical issues that need immediate attention?"

6. Get feedback from them pertaining to the goals and commitments for the team. Ask, "Do they need adjustments? Do they need to be deleted? Why?"

7. "How do you believe you are performing overall?"

8.  This next question is a very uncomfortable one but should be asked as well. "Do you feel that you're avoiding any of your responsibilities as a leader?"

Again, be cognizant to not take charge of the meeting. Be a facilitator. Some things are not up for vote, but don't let that get in the way of collaborative discussion in other areas. Teach them by influencing and guiding them to come up with their own ideas and solutions.

## An Inside Job

Did you know that 71% of employers value emotional intelligence over traditional IQ?[11] In the corporate world, they look for leaders who have the ability to collaborate, be empathetic, and communicate effectively. It's no longer just about learning the job, it's about the connection between people.

Corporate America is beginning to see how critical emotional intelligence is when it comes to leadership. Consequently, if you don't instill these core values in the current generation, not only will your players be ineffective leaders on your team, but they'll also be set up to fail in the real world.

As a coach, I'm sure you've coached a small number of innately great leaders. While great leaders might seem like a rarity, the truth is it doesn't have to be this way. It's possible to have great leaders every year, which will make your job easier, the program stronger, and your players better people.

While you can certainly try to lecture them about leadership and see what happens, I guarantee they'll more than likely understand the concepts of honesty, loyalty, and courage with ease. Unfortunately, it probably won't change a thing. This kind of systemic problem can only be fixed where the problem originates—within the heart. Otherwise, the work you do will be in quicksand because the yearning they must fill their emptiness will be too strong.

## Why Don't You Like Yourself?

One day while I was passing through the gym during a physical education class, I spotted one of my players with a group of his friends. Even though I was about 30 feet away, I could see that they were making fun of a girl in their class.

I walked briskly up to my player and pulled him aside. Instead of beating around the bush, I said, "Why don't you like yourself very much?"

"Coach, what do you mean?"

"I saw you making fun of that girl with your friends. Do you think that was the right thing to do?" He immediately dropped his head. There was no question in his mind whether it was right or wrong.

"And yet, you did it anyway. Ok, we'll let me put it this way," I went on. "When you ignore a core value that's important to you because you desire to fit in, that indicates that there must be something you dislike about yourself. To ignore anything so authentically important to your heart eventually pays a heavy toll on your self-worth. If you weren't consciously or unconsciously looking for validation from others to feel loved, you would've told them to stop—and you would have felt proud of yourself afterwards."

He was stunned, and I knew how he felt because I've been through it too. I've lost myself too many times to count. I watched as the tears welled up in his eyes.

"Listen, I want you to like yourself. And I want you to be ok with being yourself. But that starts with discovering who you really are."

Empty may be a strong word, but people who aren't empty don't need the social fulfillment that comes from teasing others. They get that fulfillment internally instead. If you implement the concepts put forth in this book, you'll be amazed at how quickly change can occur. Additionally, everything I'm outlining (love, acceptance, selflessness, etc.) creates a solid foundation for great leadership.

I think you'll find that as you continue to push forward these concepts, your team will become much better at being honest and verbalizing why they have this strong desire to belong. Take my team as an example. They were dead set against being vulnerable when I first met them, but I know if we did this type of exercise with them today, they would be willing to share what they feel without hesitation.

## Take Stock

There's a saying in AA that goes, "To thine own self be true," adopted from *Hamlet*. It requires you to not only be brutally honest with yourself, but also to identify the things in your heart that are of value to you. This is what you and your players should strive for.

Do you want to add something to your program that would create leaders? It's not enough to rely on luck. I'm sure you have plenty of players that want to be leaders but can't find the way. Even if a player wants to be a leader and loves the sport, being a leader won't be possible until you work on yourself first. When a player has things holding them back like social media, a hyper-fixation on college, or societal expectations, they don't have the tools they need to succeed.

Is it easy? *No.* And is it uncomfortable? *Absolutely.* Will you get anywhere if you don't do an inside job? You might, but the chances of that happening are much slimmer. When I walk down the hallway and see Harry, George, and Jenny, and one is Black, one is White, and one is gay, I can't help but be proud as they smile back at me. They all know I care about them for their authentic selves, not just as basketball players.

The leadership style I teach at Elite Performance Too-E is the same one I utilize. As a leader, I care about their hard work and appreciate them for it. I know I'm better equipped to influence and motivate them in a more powerful way if they're aware that I care about who they are as a person. But I can only do that by caring about myself too.

Otherwise, I can't genuinely portray to my team that I love them if I don't love myself. So, if you want to create your own leaders rather than wait for them to come along, you must be willing to go to the uncomfortable places, learn to love yourself, and teach your team to love each other. I promise it will be worth the investment.

# CHAPTER NINE

# SELFLESSNESS SELFISHNESS

## PUSHING YOUR TEAM TO A NEW LEVEL OF EXCELLENCE

Having done workshops for many athletic teams over the years, I've noticed that players often bring up selfishness. As a result, I have become very cognizant to what appears to be an alarming trend of widespread selfishness in today's athletics and society. But how did we get here? Is it because sports have shifted the focus from being a part of a team to something more individualistic?

As we've uncovered in this book, the answer can be found in to-day's definition of athlete. Being an athlete means something entirely different than what it used to mean. Today, athlete is synonymous with accolades. Instant gratification, peer approval, and money are more important than anything else. Adult influence has taken away the ability for players to connect with each other. One could even say athletics has become the new stock market.

But even with all of this going on, I stand by the idea that the self-ishness we see today isn't done with bad intentions. This is due to my belief that people aren't inherently evil, and is instead a learned behavior. On one hand, this makes it extremely hard to expel. When a person has been socialized to act a certain way and value certain things, it takes hard work to reverse this behavior. On the other hand, there's reason for optimism. If something is taught, it can also be untaught. It's not easy, but we wouldn't be in this line of work if we weren't up for a challenge, right?

## The Problem with Today

Sometimes when I walk into a workshop, I won't say hello. I don't do this to be rude or standoffish, but instead do it as an experiment. More often than not, the players don't greet me at all. Not even a simple hello. I also always leave my workshops last, which prompts me to hold the door open for the players as they file out. Ninety-five percent of the time they don't say thank you.

Think about this. Have you ever had to beg a player to try out for a team because they don't see any benefit in participating unless they're getting something out of it for themselves? In my opinion, I think this is a major reason why participation has decreased in high school sports by 43,395 players in 2018–2019.[12]

Over the years, I've had several athletes communicate to me that they realize they made a selfish play just to draw attention to themselves, knowing that it negatively impacted the team. Selfishness has produced players that are egocentric in real-time and do so even if it means losing. Society has taught children to be so self-absorbed that they don't know how to accept these acts of kindness, nor how to return them. They haven't been trained to do so.

Stop for a moment to let that sink in. Can you imagine not knowing what to do with an act of kindness? How to react to it? It baf-
fles me. I remember growing up and witnessing the importance of
manners and politeness all the time. It was abnormal for people to
*not* exhibit that kind of behavior toward others. I certainly don't
blame anyone for the behavior of kids today. Not the athletes, not
the parents, and not the coaches. I know it's due to a bigger cultural shift. But it's still a problem that needs to be fixed.

So, let me ask you, how many times have your players glossed over
a thank you? How many times has your team haphazardly cleaned
up after themselves? Been a bad friend? Been disrespectful to you?
Exhibited destructive behavior?

The number may be too high to count. And if all the above are
true, how can we expect our athletes to play selflessly on the court
if they can't be selfless off it? Selfless play is what takes a team to
the next level. It's what causes them to play until the buzzer, and to
fight for each other like their lives depend on it. Even more importantly, it's what causes these kids to become better people. This is
why it's critical that you introduce selflessness into your program.

## Learning How to Be an Athlete the Right Way

Tre' Gammage is an extraordinary young man who I've hired to
speak to my team. He uses his story to help inspire others, which
includes overcoming many personal challenges before going on
to play D1 football at Miami University in Ohio, own a highly
successful business, and author a book. As a Black man, he's a
great role model for my high school program, which is predominantly Black.

Over a six-week period, he did 12 one-hour sessions with my team he called, "Every Decision Counts: 8 Lessons I Wish They Had Taught Me in School." In one of these sessions, he said to the boys, "You guys are blessed to have a coach with the level of care and love yours has for you. There are many coaches who would never consider doing this kind of work."

I don't bring this up to self-indulge. Instead, I bring it up to highlight how great of a need there is for the work outlined in this book. Just know, as Tre's words imply, that you're validated in your desire to bring sports back to a deeper root. In the end, you're doing a good thing. But what's even more satisfying is the fact that the kids want it too. I've asked my teams before, "How many of you walked in the locker room today with the intention of helping your teammates become better people? How would it feel if other players came up to you with the same intention?"

I always hear back, "That would be amazing. But is that possible?"

As you now know, it's completely possible. First, make the distinction between selflessness and self-improvement for your athletes. Just because your players are learning selflessness doesn't mean that they should sacrifice becoming excellent in who they are. Instead, selflessness entails using one's unique talents to serve others. If you don't outline this, they may get confused and think being selfless means foregoing all self-improvement.

To begin, you need to talk about the concept of serving others. Below is an exercise you can try with your team:

1. Start a session with some open-ended questions like these: What are the benefits of serving others? What would that

mean for you as an athlete? Why would one want to go out of their way to serve others?

2. Break them into small groups of three or four to brainstorm answers.

3. Bring the team together to discuss what each group came up with.

Share with your team that if they're authentically selfless, good deeds will come back to them tenfold. I know this seems a little contradictory because one should just be kind for the sake of being kind, but you have to remember that they've been conditioned to act individualistically. You need to motivate them with this in mind.

At this point, you should also express the reasons why selflessness is important in athletics. I believe it's necessary because sports have become all about personal success, making it a fear-based experience. Spending time caring about someone else's triumphs is a non-starter. This is my explanation for the necessity of selflessness, but you can also have your own reasons, as is the case with every teaching in this book.

To get your students to see the benefit of selflessness, continue the session.

1. How does selflessness present opportunities for you that you wouldn't have had otherwise?

2. Break them into small groups to discuss.

3. Converse as a team.

Because selflessness propels a person to reach out to others, it exposes them to hundreds of people they never would've met if they remained in their individual bubble. These acts of compassion may manifest in a job, a mentorship, a lifelong friend, or simply a shoulder to cry on. The possibilities really are endless.

Currently, your athletes are likely stuck with selfish friends because they're attracting that energy like a magnet. Then, when a player needs some support, their friends will be gone the moment they really need it. Furthermore, they won't be generous enough to provide a beneficial opportunity because they'll want to keep it for themselves. The cycle of selflessness will come to a screeching halt before it even has a chance to get started.

Resume your selflessness workshop by turning words into action.

1.  Ask your team this: "What are the things we could do to express selflessness with each other, with your school, community, and family?"

2.  Break them into small groups.

3.  Discuss their answers, writing down all their ideas on the board.

4.  Because the list can be overwhelming, have your players vote on the top three most impactful things they could start doing tomorrow.

Remember, becoming selfless doesn't mean you or your players need to start a non-profit or save the world. Your team's selfless acts can be as simple as saying thank you when someone opens the door or cheering for teammates when they're doing sprints. Remind your players of this. Sometimes we think we need to be the next Messiah to be truly selfless, but the reality is much simpler.

Now it's time to show your players that selflessness already exists within them.

1. Have your players write down on a piece of paper three selfless acts they have executed in their lives, what motivated them to execute the selfless acts, and what good came out of executing the selfless acts.

2. Break the players up into groups to share with their teammates what they wrote down.

3. Bring the team together and have each group share what was discussed within the group, and what they may have learned from the exercise.

4. Write on the whiteboard key words that you hear to help establish the selflessness you want to engrain in the program.

5. Later on, use these words to create events, drills, and exercises that reinforce selflessness. For example, I've had players go into the locker room just to file out one-by-one as one of their teammates holds open the door. As each player exits, they say "thank you," while the player holding the door open would say, "you're welcome."

When your team shares their selfless acts with the group, wonderful stories of humanity start to pour out. These are stories that your athletes probably never would've shared with the team otherwise. This will connect the team to a much greater level.

I remember a particularly moving story from a player about the strong bond he had with his brother. He expressed that his older brother had been in and out of prison most of his life but was now trying to teach him to not make the same mistakes. This athlete wanted to make him proud by following his advice and not going down the same path.

After hearing this story, I asked, "Why is your connection with him so strong? What's underneath all of that?"

"My love for my brother."

"Why do you love your brother? What's one of the biggest contributing factors?"

"Because of everything he does for me." He smiled. "His selflessness." That's the *aha!* moment.

Wrap up this workshop by establishing a system of accountability:

1. Return to the three circled things your team will start doing tomorrow to be selfless.

2. Ask whether the team wants to hold each other accountable for executing these selfless acts. If they do, establish what players on the team will own overseeing this goal.

3. Create a poster spelling out what was decided and hang it in the locker room so they see it every day.

4. From time to time, have the players read the poster in the locker room as a reminder of what they committed to for each other.

Take my word for it. It's beautiful to watch these discussions take place, especially between boys. There's nothing more rewarding than watching two young men talk to each other in an intimate way despite all the societal and gendered expectations that tell them not to. The noise amongst the groups is absolutely deafening, but in the best of ways. Sometimes, it's hard for me to wrap my head around the fact that they're talking about love, empathy, and the meaning of life instead of girls, boys, school, gossip, and what they've seen on social media. And I'm constantly surprised by and proud of what they come up with.

All of this makes you realize that they're not stupid, naïve, or unaware—they've just been shut off. It's our job to turn them back on by providing the necessary guidance and stepping out of the way when we're not needed. Kevin always emphasized the importance of stepping back and observing, rather than intervening. During long talks over cups of coffee when my brother would often impart his wisdom to me, he once explained that you can't preach to a person and expect to make a lasting impact.

At the café we frequented, Kevin looked into his cup of coffee as if he was reading the universe in it—and I always suspected he actually could be. After glancing at me, he said, "It doesn't matter how great of a speaker you think you are. If you're lecturing a group of players, you'll be lucky if they listen for more than five minutes. You might think you were exceptional, but within a few days, or even a few hours, the players will be back to behaving in the same manner. Now tell me, who is all of this about? You or the kids?"

"The kids," I said.

He downed what remained in his cup in one final gulp. "Exactly."

If you speak on a pedestal, your athletes will never be invested in what you're teaching. They need to be included in the conversation and create their own solutions. They need to think for themselves instead of blindly following a blueprint handed down to them by their parents and society.

Let them be a part of the answer. When that happens, they'll finally have the potential to shift their behavior and overall way of thinking.

## The Psychology of Today

To grasp why selflessness is important, it may be beneficial to understand how the cultural shift I've discussed has negatively affected altruism.

One day during practice, I decided to set up a drill based on trust and selflessness. Players would take turns coaching two of their fellow teammates. The intention of this training was to show generosity and give another person their undivided attention. One by one, the players took turns switching through the role of coach and player. Eventually, when an athlete named Joe was asked to take his turn to coach, I watched with disappointment as he spent the drill going through the motions. He was completely void of care and emotion.

During the break, I pulled him aside and said, "Joe, you were empty out there. Why do you think that was?"

"Honestly," he murmured back, "I just didn't care."

I shook my head with disbelief. Sometimes it's hard to imagine having that kind of apathy. Even in my darkest days, I was selfless and caring because I was taught to be that way. So, I asked, "Why not?"

He responded with brevity. "Because I've never had to do anything like that before."

I dug again. "Help me understand how you got to that point. Why have you never done anything like that before?"

"Because," he said, scratching his head, "I've never been asked to."

Joe has the capacity to care, love, and want the best for his teammates. All his behavior told me was that we need to continue to find ways to help people connected to that gift. Kids have been socialized to always ask themselves, *How can this benefit me?* If they're not playing, the sport isn't worth it anymore. Can it get any more selfish than abandoning a team, despite all the relationships they've formed through it, because there's nothing of value to them other than playing?

There are too many people who aren't connected to or are aware of the benefits, life lessons, and significance athletic experiences bring. Far too often, these ideas are just lip service, and there's no intent to integrate or teach within the program. And as I mentioned before, the lack of manners shows a lack of empathy. When you're greeting someone, holding the door open, or thanking someone, you must have a sense of selflessness because you're recognizing there's someone other than yourself in that moment.

Selfishness is also a reason for the emptiness that some youth feel. When an individual achieves just for themselves, they reach their final destination alone. That's why there can sometimes be a sinking feeling that can make a person ask, *Is this all there is?* As we all know, it's not about the destination, but the journey and the people you meet along the way.

Unfortunately, I believe this cultural shift is a source of harm, and coaching is one area that needs to be looked at. Some coaches may find themselves being more selfish than they ever imagined they could be, and it's something that's rooted in our individualistic culture.

When I observed a meeting between a coach and his players during the offseason while the program was holding optional practice and training, one of the players who frequently missed practices due to his AAU season rushed into the meeting five minutes late. His hair was wet and his clothes were hastily thrown on. He was clearly coming from another AAU practice.

"Sorry, Coach," he mumbled with tiredness in his voice, then took a seat next to one of his friends. I glanced at the coach to observe his reaction and saw his head drop. He took a deep breath. *Don't go there*, I said to myself, knowing my silent prayers were worthless.

His cheeks flushed with anger. "If you miss any more practices, your chances of playing next season are going to be slim."

I took a deep breath in, then let it go. These kinds of reactions are to be expected. In fact, I've had my fair share of them. I know it's not said with ill intent, but it's still dangerous to imply these sentiments to the team. Specifically, you're sending mixed signals, playing with emotions, using fear-based tactics, and threats of punishments that shouldn't exist. After the meeting, I asked to speak to the coach in private because I didn't want to put him on the spot or embarrass him in front of his team.

"Listen," I said. "You can't communicate to a player that if he misses something optional, he will be chastised for it." His eyes sunk to the ground. He immediately understood his error. "Coach, let me tell you something." I rested a hand on his shoulder for reassurance, and his eyes met mine. "Here's the goal. You should want that kid to choose to come to your practices over the AAU practices because your program gives him more. The goal you want to achieve is that your program becomes a program of attraction."

And that should be your goal for your program too. Because kids today have been steered away from a meaningful athletic experience, they won't be able to detail what's special about your program from any other. Some people think the sessions we do are a ludicrous form of therapy. I don't agree with those sentiments at all, but I do think there's one important similarity between therapy and what we do, because we are helping people.

People can call all of this whatever they want, but know that it's absolutely necessary. Your athletes likely have dysfunctional and destructive tendencies. Those ailments need attention, whether that be in the form of therapy or something else. You can't scream the dysfunction out of someone.

It's true that the methods in this book, which evolved as a result of my work through Elite Performance Too-E, may not work for everyone. But if they can help at least *one person*—that should be enough motivation to give them a try. It's time to stop cheating athletes, coaches, and yourself from a life-changing experience.

## The True Meaning of Success

Having the opportunity to teach selflessness, as you do, is a rare and important act that has the potential to cause a chain reaction.

Your players will begin to separate themselves from others as leaders because their inner beauty and talents will allow them to stand out. And here comes the best part. They'll be more likely to go out into the world, be difference-makers, and teach selflessness to others. This is what we truly need in the world today.

Because we're in this position, we're able to do something that wouldn't have been possible in many other vocations and shape the lives of these young men and women in a positive way. I know that what I've been discussing has nothing to do with championships. But it does have everything to do with the common good, humanity, and the world.

John Wooden knew the heart of an athlete was more important than their output as a player, as demonstrated when he said, "Winning takes talent, to repeat takes character."[13] This was a concept he integrated throughout his Pyramid of Success.[14]

Wooden was aware of the fact that he was given an opportunity to help people grow into world-changing individuals. He wasn't going to make it a shallow experience for them or squander the opportunity by wasting time on 1,000 drills.

This is a philosophy I try to take to heart, and you should too.

# CHAPTER TEN

# H.O.W. TO CHANGE

Every team has problems, but in many instances, they come in varying forms of severity. When you ignore problems, it only makes matters worse, as they'll eventually grow and destroy a team from the inside out. This is why it's important to address them as soon as possible.

As Kevin used to say, "You can't just sweep it under the carpet and pretend it's not there." As coaches and leaders, it's our responsibility to upholster the carpet and expose what's underneath—even if a player is scoring 22 points a game. You can do that by following the teachings outlined in this book, but let's be honest, it won't work without a way to implement them.

That's where H.O.W. comes in. H.O.W. is an acronym that stands for *honesty*, *owning*, and *willingness*. It's a simple methodology for change that actually works, and is one that I picked up during my recovery from alcoholism. So what the heck does all this mean?

Let me break down H.O.W. by explaining each step and using my experiences as an example.

# An Introduction

*Honesty* is just the beginning, but it's an extremely crucial step. If a player is incapable of being honest with themselves about their shortcomings, none of the other steps matter. For a long time, I refused to admit my drinking habits weren't normal, because that would mean I was weak and abnormal. I couldn't acknowledge what I knew deep down in my heart, so I justified it by associating with people who also liked to drink. It wasn't until I was thoroughly honest with myself about being an alcoholic that I had an opportunity to do something about it.

*Owning* is where finally change has a chance. It occurs after honest reflection is executed and the discoveries it brings are recognized as truth. This step is all about taking responsibility for what needs improvement. Many people tend to blame their problems and shortcomings on others or their environment. I know I did this too. Eventually, I was able to claim my alcoholism, even though I used to believe that any other person who lived my life would've drank just as much as me.

*Willingness* is the third step and is an invitation to take action. It happens when change stops becoming a thought and becomes a commitment. At this juncture, one has an opportunity to truly begin the process of personal improvement. The benefit of an invitation to take action is that it eliminates the scenario where many people rebel when they're told what they need to do. But there's a catch. In order to be willing to change, willingness needs to be seen in one's actions. Unlike the other steps, willingness is a decision that must be continuously made every single day.

There's another reason why this step is the most challenging. Sometimes, the habits we've built up over the years are too strong to break right away. Instead, they need to be chipped at over time. There was a point in my journey where I was able to say, "Yes, I'm an alcoholic and it's no one's fault but my own, but I'm still going to drink this way, and no one is going to change that."

The antidote required for a player to open up is imperative to this process. First and foremost, players need nonjudgment and empathy. Without it, your players will shut down and aren't likely to get past the first step. Nonjudgment and empathy have the ability to break down a person's protective armor so that self-reflection can happen.

Introduce these concepts by reminding players that no one is perfect. Consequently, by instilling this thought process athletes will feel safe to be more vulnerable and be excited to "fall forward"—one of my favorite sayings by actor Denzel Washington.[15] They'll stop interpreting their shortcomings as flaws and instead think of them as opportunities to grow.

## Where to Begin

Change is a scary word, and the process can be quite intimidating. But if you follow this easy guide, you'll be well on your way to helping your athletes. Remember *distractions*, that 25-word list I discussed in chapter two?

1.  Create a list again on the whiteboard, but this time comprise it of shortcomings like selfishness, anger, jealousy, envy, dishonesty, hate, and so on.

2.  Place the players in groups of three and ask each student to jot down the top three things they could work on. Include a short statement about how each of the shortcomings are destructive or hurtful to them. Here, they can begin to see why self-improvement is needed.

3.  Instruct your athletes to share what they've written down aloud in their small groups.

4.  Have your players return to their list and write down a strong, motivating statement that will keep them committed to changing their shortcomings. This should include what benefits they will gain if they achieve self-improvement. When they're done, have each player share what they wrote down with their teammates.

5.  Lastly, have each player communicate whether they give their teammates permission to hold them accountable to the changes they want to make.

This process is useful because it requires them to be honest with themselves. Just keep in mind that sometimes we aren't aware of our faults. For example, a player raised his hand during a session and asked, "If I cheat on my girlfriend and don't get caught, that's not cheating, right?" He was sincerely asking.

We're all products of our environment, so we believe certain things are normal. For this player, his home environment may have taught him this kind of behavior is ok. He may also have trouble looking at his actions and truthfully understanding that they're destructive.

When a particular athlete is having trouble being honest with themselves, you can open the discussion up to his teammates as long as the player permits it and the teammates come from a place of nonjudgement. Their teammates will likely point to areas of the player's behavior that hurts the team. Most times, players will come out of the session grateful that they're aware of shortcomings they've honestly never seen in themselves.

When everyone is done with their small group work, bring the entire team back together for the second exercise.

Communicate to the group that the upcoming exercise is not about anyone giving advice, trying to fix them, or pass judgement on the person who's sharing.

Direct each player to stand up and share their list with the team.

After everyone has shared, open the discussion. Ask, "What was it like to hear from all the players? How did it affect you? What did it reveal to you? What were you feeling when you heard what was being shared?"

The exercise above will help a player become more connected and conscious of their shortcomings, and when a player is more connected to the truth of their shortcomings, they'll be more motivated to change.

For the next and final exercise, get your team back into their small groups again.

Have players write down the actions and steps they need to take to begin changing the shortcomings they revealed.

Then, tell them to share their actions and steps with the other players in their unit.

Just like before, after the small group work is done bring the team back together again and have each player share their actions and steps with the whole team.

Once the player is done sharing, ask them if they would like to hear suggested actions and steps from their teammates. If the player says yes, it's imperative that you communicate to the team to only share actions and steps and to not give advice on how to fix the problem. If the player says no, move onto the next player.

Finally, after verbalizing their list, give the player the option to express whether he or she gives their teammates permission to hold them accountable for the steps and actions needed to make a change. I always ask that the player take some time to seriously consider their answer. If they say yes, there's a possibility that they will receive feedback that's difficult to hear but will help them immensely. There's nothing more motivating than not wanting to let your family down!

Congratulations! After doing this training, you'll have laid the foundation for accountability to take place. Just remember that throughout the year, there's no doubt that most player's shortcomings will come up again. That's why there's truth in the saying *two steps forward, one step back*. But the beauty of this exercise is that you've already gotten the entire team involved and committed to the work, so it softens the defensive armor a player may have put up when being called out. In other words, they're all in it together.

Now, I know what you may be thinking... *This is some kind of thera-py! Why should I make this huge effort to fit this in?* I'm an extremely competitive coach, so I wouldn't do these things if they didn't help a team to win. There's no metric to measure the effect H.O.W. has on an individual or team, but I have seen *magical* results time and time again. The team will start to function as one seamless unit and there will be less drama and more trust. They'll be playing out of love, which is the most powerful fuel known to humankind.

## It's Not My Fault

Let's see how H.O.W. works in action (see what I did there?).

I was hired to work with a high school baseball team to do several workshops. Immediately after accepting the job, I was introduced to Seth, who was at risk of being kicked off the baseball team *and* out of school for his grades. He was in the middle of a summer semester when I was hired. Reports flooded in from his teachers detailing how he regularly skipped classes, didn't turn in any work, and made constant excuses.

It took one day to understand the magnitude of this case. While sitting in the principal's office with the athletic director, principal, Seth, and his father, it was communicated to Seth that he was failing all his courses. It also became clear that if Seth missed any more classes, he would not pass. Seth and his father knew exactly what was at stake after that meeting.

The following day, the assistant coach waited at school all morning to make sure Seth was in attendance. He never showed up. The assistant coach quickly dialed Seth's home phone number. His father picked up and explained that he didn't know where Seth was, but that he would check his bedroom. After a minute of pure silence, his father got back on the line and said, "He's still sleeping."

The assistant coach and I theorized a plan. Our first realization was that we wouldn't be able to do a thing for Seth if he didn't make it through summer school. Most of the work would need to happen during the school year when we had more time with him. At the moment, it was decided that we needed to be more engaged in helping him pass his summer classes so that he would be eligible to return to school in the fall.

During the summer, we kept in contact with the athletic director, principal, and Seth's teachers to monitor his attendance and performance. We checked in with Seth frequently to make sure he was completing his assignments on time. The assistant coach even offered to pick him up in the mornings and give him a ride to school, even though he only lived a 15-minute walk away. The funny thing is, you would've thought he had to walk halfway across the world based on his response whenever he used not having a ride as an excuse.

Thankfully, Seth made it through summer school and made it to the fall without much of a hiccup. During one of our first team workshops, I did the H.O.W. exercise with Seth. If I'm being honest, this wasn't his primary issue. He easily acknowledged school was his biggest hurdle. But when I asked him, "What is it about school that's so challenging?" he would describe obstacles that had nothing to do with him. The excuses would range from his father not waking him up in the mornings to the alarm on his phone not going off to his teachers not being helpful enough.

The most concerning part about all of this was the complete apathy I sensed from him. It seemed like he just didn't have any interest in changing his attitude toward academics. The only thing we had as motivational leverage was his desire to be a part of the baseball program.

"I just really can't do it, Coach Touhey," was the statement he left me with.

Because he wouldn't take ownership of his actions, I pushed back. When pressing a player like this, it's important to clarify that you aren't being hard on them to scold, reprimand, or punish them. Your only desire is to help them because you care for them. After noting the above, I said, "I've heard a lot about others and your environment, but what are you doing to contribute to this problem? Do you think you have any part in this?"

Always pay attention to language. Seth started to use the word *I*. He went on to explain that he couldn't get out of bed in the morning because he was up until all hours of the night.

"I am just curious. What does your father, phone, teacher, and distance to school have to do with you staying up most of the night?" I questioned.

*They have nothing to do with it.*

"Interesting," I replied. "Then, would it be safe to say that the primary reason you don't go to school or do your homework is that you choose to stay up most of the time?"

*Yes.*

"And how is that benefitting you? What skillset is that bringing you?"

*It's not helping me at all.*

It was a breakthrough. Seth finally began to own his behavior. I asked him to write down the reasons why he does things that set him up for failure, then told him to share this information verbally to his teammates. This was not so they could ridicule him, but so they could begin to understand him.

After hearing his perspective, I said, "Seth, if you're willing, could we ask your teammates how they feel about your actions, and how it affects them?" Sometimes, players prefer not to open it up to the room and I respect that, but in this case, Seth said yes. I emphasized to the room that their thoughts needed to be stated with nonjudgment because, in reality, all of us have shortcomings we may or may not be aware of.

Seth's teammates offered encouraging words, said they could help out and give him rides to school, and one even said they would work with him to create a schedule for his homework. The overwhelming sentiment was that they sincerely believed in him. When the room settled down, I shared with Seth what I had observed. After repeating a pattern of destructive behaviors, he convinced himself that he was not capable of succeeding. But then I told him the truth. That he was no dummy, that he was a brilliant young man, and capable of anything. "I believe this," I said. "And, clearly, so does everyone else here."

And he started to believe in himself too. During that season, Seth began to change. At one point, he even told me that he was determined to get no lower than a letter grade of "C" on his report card. That's not to say there weren't roadblocks. Two steps forward, one step back. He was suspended from playing a few games because he was falling behind in his classes. But thankfully, I knew the work we'd done with Seth, and the result was a deeper connection with his teammates and coaching staff. They would not let him quit on himself again. The old Seth would've most likely walked away from school and baseball.

That gave us all hope and created a connection of love for him throughout the program. After a season of ups and downs but general progress, Seth's final summer school came knocking on the door—and he answered. He was the first in line to sign up for classes without anyone telling him to do so. He was the first to finish all his work in class. After completing all the necessary classes, he even met with the principal to sign up for more classes.

The principal was shocked at his transformation. Today, his report card has Bs and Cs instead of being littered with Ds and Fs like it was in the past. Seth's story isn't finished yet. School and baseball season will come around again, which will require him to balance even more things. However, I know he will walk across that stage in his cap and gown because he has a ray of hope, and it's all because he's starting to truly love himself.

## Why We Refuse to Change

In the middle of a session with Seth, I asked him, "What are you so afraid of?"

His response surprised me. "If I change who I am, that means I have to change everything. I won't be the same person to my friends, my parents, or my teachers. They'll expect something of me, but it's easier to live without expectations. In fact, having them scares the living daylights out of me."

Seth was experiencing the comfort level that comes with failure. It's something I had been all too familiar with when I was young.

But for many, their hesitance to change may come from a plethora of reasons. For example, they may need help being completely honest with themselves. Others have convinced themselves they were predestined to have a difficult life, believe they're a victim of circumstance, or build their lives on a foundation of negativity. Some, as is the case in this next instance, won't want to do the hard work required to change until they realize how their actions are hurting others. Understanding these reasons will help you learn how to best serve your players.

## Ownership Does Not Equal Change

Several years ago, I was doing Elite Performance Too-E workshops for a girl's high school basketball program. Two of the better players on the team were extremely selfish and angry. Sue was the starting point guard, and Cheryl was the starting small forward. For now, let's focus on Sue's story.

Sue was the type of player who would walk off the court in the middle of a pickup game if she didn't like how it was going. She had gone through two coaches and quit the team the prior two seasons. Whenever the team lost, she would chuck the basketball across the court and storm off the floor. At the time, I knew she was going to be a difficult case.

During a H.O.W. workshop, I asked her what areas she could improve in. She had no trouble answering.

"Coach, I know sometimes I have major anger issues and I can be selfish." Meanwhile, I thought, *Well, at least we can skip that part of the exercise,* and I moved on. "Would it be hard to own any of that?"

Again, she had no trouble answering. "Not hard at all, Coach. That's just who I am." *Breezed through that one too*, I thought. If this was a test, she would've been acing it. However, what Sue was having a problem with was difficult to tackle. It was her unwillingness to evolve that caused her the most trouble, though a lack of trust was also an issue that would need to be resolved. It caused her to put up a protective shield of anger to ward off anyone from getting too close.

But the thing was, Sue's temper affected those around her in ways she was blind to. After I received her permission in a workshop, I opened the conversation up to her teammates to express the pain Sue may have caused them. The consensus was they were afraid to make mistakes around her, they couldn't trust her even though she was the best player and thought of as the team leader, and they didn't want to be near her.

Hearing all of this was very painful and difficult for Sue—especially because three of the players that spoke up were her closest friends. Listening to the hurt in her teammate's voices turned on a switch of empathy that Sue liked to keep off. You could see the defeat in her eyes and the subsequent reflection. I asked, "Now let me ask you this. How willing are you to change?"

This is a big moment in these kinds of sessions. It's where the rubber meets the road. If the player isn't willing, then there's nothing you can do for them, and they won't be on the team much longer. It's just not fair to the other players who want to be an actual family. I cautioned her before letting her respond.

"Before you respond, I want you to know that we care about you very much. However, I can't sit around and let you self-destruct and destroy this family while you're at it. Even though we all love you, hard decisions must be made. Are you willing to do that?"

She said yes, and together we created an action plan for Sue that would guide her through the year. There were three months to lay a new foundation for her before practices started. Luckily, by the time October rolled around, she had shown some serious improvement.

Before the ninth game into the season, Sue pulled me aside. "I want to show you something," she said, and pulled out a piece of paper tucked in her sock. It said the word *patience* on it. This may seem very minor, but this was big for Sue. It was a testament to her evolution. This was a kid who went from cursing aloud and storming off the floor in pickup games to writing what she needed to work on the piece of paper she tucked into her sock because she thought it was important enough to do so. For me, the word on that paper symbolized her action and commitment.

## The Boiling Point

There's always a moment in every person's transformation when they hit rock bottom. This usually occurs just before showing the greatest amount of growth or they give up completely. Sue reached this point during a game later in the season. During a timeout, the assistant coaches gave Sue some instruction and coaching points. She didn't take it well and decided to leave the bench and disappear into the locker room. I received a call from the head coach that evening, who explained what happened. He asked if I would come in to work with Sue. I got on a flight two days later.

I'll admit I wasn't in the best mindset on my flight out. I was upset, angry, and disappointed. How could she have come so far just to erupt like that? She hadn't just taken two steps back—she'd taken six. And to be honest, I was going to suggest to the head coach that she be kicked off the team because, selfishly, I didn't want to work with her any longer.

But then as always, I took a deep breath and let out my frustrations. I reminded myself why I do this kind of work, what I owed to kids like Sue. Then I thought about what my brother would do. I recalled the piece of paper she'd tucked away in her sock and everything it signified. If she hadn't shown me she was trying, it would have been an easy decision for me to inform the head coach that she was not going to change. Instead, I reached out to Sue to set up a meeting.

## Surviving Without the Stars

"What do you think needs to be done?" I asked her. We were sitting in an empty locker room, surrounded by unwashed jerseys and basketball shoes.

"I need to apologize to Coach and the team," she said with a confidence in her voice that proved her authenticity and regret. She went on to explain how she felt in that moment, how she'd been so consumed by anger that she couldn't let go. She admitted that she knew she was making a mistake the second she walked off the court and even considered turning around and apologizing, except her pride wouldn't let her.

Sue showed some great awareness that day. Although she messed up, she proved to me that her character was in the process of growing. The head coach ended up giving her the same penalty as Cheryl, the other player who had been acting out in a similar manner. They were suspended for the next three games and weren't allowed to show their faces at practice or sit on the bench during games. It just so happened that those next three games were some of the school's toughest of the year.

Even with two of their starting players gone, I knew the team was up for a challenge and wasn't worried for them. Time and time again, I've been reminded of how much a team can improve when distractions are gone—especially when those distractions come in the form of starters whose character flaws have been overlooked for the sake of winning.

The community thought the coach was crazy for benching two of her better players, but she proved everyone wrong within the first four minutes of the game. On the offensive end, the players were moving the ball and making the extra pass like never before. They were winning battles for loose balls by diving on the floor. Players that were normally afraid of taking shots were scoring. On the defensive end, their rotations were fast and crisp, their box outs more intentional. To top it all off, the support and encouragement coming from the bench fueled the team up with a confidence they'd never played with before.

Because of the elimination of the drain and drag that was being created by two of the better players in the program, the team was finally able to perform at an elevated level. Their primary drive became not wanting to let their family down. They were truly an embodiment of Kevin's beliefs. He would've been proud. And even though they lost by three points, the team wasn't angry or upset. They were disappointed, sure, but since they played for each other and left nothing on the court, and for that they could be proud of what they'd accomplished.

When the second game came around, the same thing happened. Even though they were clearly outmatched, the other team scraped by with a win. Sue and Cheryl were watching from the stands in disbelief. I even heard the referee say, "Coach, I've never seen a team work so hard."

Later that evening, Sue texted me to ask if I would talk to the head coach about allowing her and Cheryl to sit on the bench for the last game of their suspension. They wanted to be a part of the team again, regardless of whether they were playing or not. The head coach allowed them to come, and I'm glad she did.

During that last game, Sue and Cheryl displayed more passion on the bench than they ever had on the court. They were cheering the girls on, hugging them as they walked off the floor during time-outs, and giving them water bottles the moment they sat down. With just three and a half minutes left in the game, the other team was up by 15 points. There was an exciting energy in the air. I sensed the girls were nervous, but relentless at the same time. They were going to fight until the final buzzer rang.

And they did.

They cut the lead to two points with just one minute remaining in the game against a team they shouldn't have a chance to compete with. When the final buzzer sounded, I smiled. I looked at Sue, who may have been bursting with anger at the loss had she been playing. Only this time, she patted the backs of her teammates and expressed how proud she was of each and every one of them.

Once they were in the locker room, I asked the head coach if I could gather the players. I remember considering that Sue and Cheryl probably thought the team was going to get crushed in their absence, but they turned out to be 20 to 30 points better without them.

After congratulating the team on their hard work, I directly addressed Sue and Cheryl. "Listen, your teammates miss you. They really do. And I want you to know that the other nine girls on this team never once told me or Coach they don't want you back, despite the very cruel things you've said about the team and coaching staff. But at the same time, their love and the mutual respect that they have for each other gave them the ability to be successful without you. I hope you find some humility in that."

I believe that stuck with them, because from that moment on, Sue and Cheryl understood what it meant to be a part of a family.

## The Strength of H.O.W.

There's great power in self-improvement. The teachings of Kevin and I at Elite Performance Too-E are rooted in the philosophy that when a player grows as a person, they become stronger in the sport because they're learning to eliminate the things that hold them back. Developing this skill is no less vital than working on ability, execution, and strategy.

If you just pretend these problems aren't there, or sweep them under the carpet as Kevin would say, they'll fester until they implode. Instead, know that investing time in your players' personal growth will lay the groundwork for a team that functions at the highest level possible. Providing and teaching tools that help players improve and grow as people creates a passionate connection to the sport that never waivers, no matter the outcome or level of adversity.

Elite Performance Too-E's mission is to influence and guide each player towards a designation of excellence to become the best possible version of themselves as people. And that's why you should never just sweep it under the carpet. Do it for the sake of your team, its spirit, and your players' future.

# CHAPTER ELEVEN

# GRATITUDE

## HEART WINS CHAMPIONSHIPS

On a particularly sunny day, I decided to take my team outside for conditioning because of the nice weather. As drills began and the boys started to sprint up and down, I shielded my eyes from the sun so I could watch. I noticed another team out on the field too, and I was shocked by what I saw.

For a football team, the attendance numbers were extremely low with only around 30 at practice. This made me think, *What happened to the program that had 140 players every year? Where are all the programs that sometimes had too many interested athletes?*

For me, this points to one of the big problems in athletics today is participation. The decline has been steady for some time now. The data shows that most kids quit sports around the age of 11,[16] and that the big four sports (baseball, basketball, football, and soccer) have been hit the hardest by the scarcity—each of them decreasing by approximately three percent from 2008 to 2016.[17]

There are several reasons why participation has dropped. Some of the biggest factors are cost and fear of injury.[18]

Unfortunately, these are things we don't always have control over as coaches. So, regardless of the reasons, the fact is fewer kids are playing. That means fewer are learning valuable life lessons, building relationships, and connecting with others, resulting in fewer lives being changed for the better.

We as coaches can't do a thing about that if there's no one left to play the game. This is why we need to wake up. Our jobs have changed. The days of putting a few flyers on bulletin boards and watching the crowds grow at tryouts isn't a feasible strategy anymore. Athletics have become a business transaction now—something that requires a *this is what we can do for you* pitch, which means you need to start selling your program. Having a winning team helps, but it's not an end-all solution anymore.

Instead, you need to turn your program into a program of attraction. This requires building a program that piques interest anytime a player or a parent talks about it and that's not based solely on winning. It may sound outlandish, but with a little hard work it's possible to develop a program of attraction through gratitude while also creating a winning culture.

## Gratitude Is the Way

It used to be the case that a winning program would attract players, but that's not really true anymore. Part of the reason is because there are so many other activities coaches have to compete against to attract players that were not around in past generations. Hell, even video games are something to compete against!

I also believe this is due to the toll it takes on a person when winning is the sole focus. In sports, we've spent so much time on the extrinsic development of skill, weight training, conditioning, and execution to produce wins that we've forgotten about the importance of intrinsic development.

Don't get me wrong—winning feels good, but it's not satisfying long-term. Moreover, not everybody wins and not every team wins. Many players I work with express that participating feels more like a burden than joy, even while they're winning. Because athletics have become a shallow experience with such an intense concentration on outcome, young players are trained to see value in these things. However, it's human nature to want more. Perhaps without even realizing it, there's a desire to connect, love, and create memorable experiences with one another. Studies show that humanity's deepest desire is to foster shared realities,[19] proving our need for interconnectivity.

What you should strive for is when others hear about your program, they'll crave what it offers, sometimes without even understanding why. Just as a service or product provides value to a customer, your program will add an immense amount of value to these kids' lives. Awakening your players to the many benefits of being a part of a team and teaching them that there's more to sports than notoriety, money, and accolades are tools they're sure to be grateful for. And the good news is, gratitude can spread through teams and communities.

I've coached basketball at our local high school for a year now and our program has become drastically different from others, and people are starting to take notice. The other day, I studied my team as they worked through a pre-season drill and was surprised when I received a tap on the shoulder. I turned around and saw two high school boys, both in gym shorts and sneakers.

"Yes?" I asked, somewhat confused. I wasn't sure if we'd met before.

"We want to play for you."

"Uh—we'd love that. Do you have any experience playing?"

"Not really," one of them replied. "The last time we played was at the YMCA in fourth grade."

What? I shook my head in disbelief. "Why do you want to play now, then? I'm just curious."

"We just heard some really great things about your program that have nothing to do with basketball. It sounds like fun."

I was completely blown away. How does something like this happen? There were two players wanting to join a sport they've never really played before. How is this possible in a time when athletic participation is steadily dropping? For me, I think the answer is gratitude. I know what my players are saying in the hallways at school and the sentiment that spreads throughout campus. They're talking about the love they have for this program, the relationships they've developed, and the care we have for them. It's the value we provide.

During one of his workshops, Tre' said to the boys, "Your coach is unique in that he hired me to work with you to be successful in life, not just basketball. It signifies his intention to help you grow as people. Now, everyone, I want to hear what you're observing in this program that's different from what you've experienced in the past. Especially from the seniors, who played for other coaches."

I sat in the corner with a smile on my face as three of our seniors jumped to the front and spoke to the underclassmen. "Coach loves us as people. He cares about what happens to us in life. He has a genuine commitment to doing everything he can for us. I've never had that in any other coach."

One player even said, "You need to listen to this man. Listen to him. I wish I had access to something like this program as a freshman."

I didn't ask for any of their kind words, and I clearly wasn't prepped for it (being that I was left teary-eyed). I'm also not bringing this up to gloat. My point is, if your players are sending that same message out into the world, that's a great return on investment, if you want to call it that. People want to be a part of our program because we're offering something different. And it's possible for you to do the same.

## Introducing Gratitude

As you start to implement the teachings in this book, gratitude may or may not come naturally. Here's a simple gratitude workshop you can do with your team to make it a bit easier to incorporate:

Ask your team what they're grateful for in the program.

Break them into small groups where they will come up with their answers.

Discuss their responses as a team. As you move around the room, going from group to group, write everyone's comments down on the whiteboard so they can witness the sheer number of things they can be grateful for.

This exercise is wonderful because of its simplicity and accessibility. There's so much to be grateful for, and all you have to do is get your team to name these things. The hope is also that through gratitude, they'll become more gracious people because they'll start to recognize how lucky they are just to have clothes on their backs and sneakers on their feet.

Additionally, they should begin to appreciate your program organically, rather than having to be reminded by their coach. The *you should be honored to wear this jersey* days are behind us, along with the days of just respecting someone with the name Coach. And maybe that's a good thing.

It's true that elders and authority deserve some respect, and this notion is still relevant but perhaps not as prevalent as it used to be. Earlier generations were taught to respect a nametag, but honestly that sometimes gives people power that didn't earn or deserve it. That kind of influence changes a person and feeds egos.

You or other coaches you know may think kids today are a pain in the ass. I don't believe that, but a big reason why they may be more defiant is that they don't trust authority. And, as I pointed out, blind trust isn't always a good thing. That's why you need to continue to find ways to connect with them every single day. Collaborate and co-create extrinsic and intrinsic goals together. Have sessions that encourage discussions involving current events or personal experiences. These kinds of discussions will bring up topics like vulnerability, compassion, and other emotions that build intimacy without you ever having to say the word.

As you do, you'll be shocked at the amount of value you can add to their lives, what they can give back, and the number of kids in pain who need this kind of help in their lives.

# The Other Side of Pain

During one of his "Lessons I Wish They Taught Me in School" sessions, Tre' asked the team to share destructive decisions they've made in the past that were wrong but did anyway because they didn't care about the consequences.

As the team spoke one by one, I shook my head in disbelief, remembering the people they used to be. These were individuals that couldn't make eye contact the first time I walked into the gym because they didn't trust me. Now, after a year of training, they shared personal experiences to their peers and coaches. This was an incredible group of 14- to 17-year-olds who had learned to listen with empathy, love, and care. It was remarkable, and more importantly, they were remarkable.

After the session ended, there was a moment of silence. It wasn't an uncomfortable one, but rather a silence that displayed how special the session had been. During those 60 seconds, a clarity came to me. I decided to share some of the deepest, darkest choices I had ever made, something only those closest to me knew.

I walked to the front of the room, grabbed a chair, and faced them.

"I got into my first serious relationship with a girl when I was 19. I didn't care about much other than drinking back then. I was also incredibly irresponsible and apathetic. Some of the decisions I made, when I was in that state of mind, were terrible. There's a part of me that hates myself for them to this day.

"I got a girl pregnant. She had an abortion. It was devastating, but not devastating enough for me to do anything about it. My drinking didn't change and my attitude didn't either. The only thing I felt was guilt and shame, but that went away over time as numbness replaced it.

"A year later, I got into another serious relationship. Over the course of our seven-year partnership, I got her pregnant twice. She had two abortions."

They were watching me with wide, surprised eyes. Sighing, I released the same tension I always felt every time I'd shared this part of me. An intense fear took hold as I grew afraid of not being accepted, of being thought of as disgusting or evil, or of never being looked at the same way by people I care about. Somehow, I mustered the courage to go on.

"I share this with you because I don't want any of you to experience something like this. There isn't a day that goes by where I don't feel a tremendous amount of pain. There isn't a day that goes by where I don't drive past a sign that says, 'Abortion is Murder,' and it doesn't send a shiver down my spine. I was reckless and didn't care about protection, and it was the ultimate form of selfishness. Ultimately, my past motivates me to serve because I have a lot to make up for. And thankfully I still have some time to do that."

You could have heard a pin drop the room was so quiet.

"I'm sorry for bringing up something that may have been too intense to hear, but I did it because I'm not unique," I said. "I know there are others out there that feel this same pain. And I know it's possible that one of you may be dealing with this situation or one like it. This is why I have a responsibility to bring it up. I just really don't want any of you to experience what I did."

Once I was done and the boys had a minute to process everything, they rushed to my side. All at once, so it was impossible to discern who was speaking. "We love you, Coach Touhey," and, "You're not a bad person, please don't be so hard on yourself." I wasn't asking for any of that, but I feel incredibly grateful that I have this kind of relationship with them. And I know they are mutually grateful for me, the coaches, and our program too.

I'm aware you may not have a story like mine, but everyone has something to share. It doesn't have to be as deep or as hard to get out. It just has to be personal, genuine, and true. It can be about love, joy, happiness, or the opposite—so long as you speak from the heart about something that matters to you.

I know sharing is never easy, but I urge you to do so. Lead by example and remember that if you don't open up, your players never will learn to do so either.

## Becoming a Program of Attraction

You may be thinking, how does any of this have anything to do with basketball? Well, we reap the benefits of the game. See, that moment of love occurred because an orange ball with black stripes brought us together. When you think about that, isn't it incredible that we're able to connect on a new level because of a ball? That we can learn about life, loss, and everything in-between because of a sport?

That's why your team should be grateful to play, and you should be grateful to coach. It allows for so much more than you could ever expect or ask for. If we're paying attention as humans, it's easy to see how much there is to be grateful for. However, your team may need some help recognizing what these things are. If you find that your group is having a difficult time with gratitude, you can aid their pursuits by showing them the beauty of athletics.

Start by discussing these topics and any other ones you may think of.

1. **Relationships**

   As people, we 're going to be in relationships our entire lives that have nothing to do with sport. They are unavoidable, which is why your team must learn what healthy relationships are. This is where athletics come in to play. Playing a team sport automatically puts these kids in close proximity to other people where relationships will form. In these relationships, they'll get chances to agree or disagree, accept disappointment, contribute, collaborate, motivate, and get to know others' perspectives. Think of it as practice for the future. And as coaches, we can observe what they're doing in these relationships, provide guidance, and highlight teachable moments.

   Beyond the relationship-training that comes with being on a team, the bond players form with each other is unique and special. Teammates are given a chance to become friends with each other and fight for one another, which is a rare opportunity. I watch my team make such a great effort to be the best they can be in their relationships every day. And they're getting these opportunities from basketball. To me, that's pretty miraculous.

2. **The Opportunity to Help Others**

   Beyond helping an individual become successful in the workforce, selflessness can make a person a better leader by helping others achieve their fullest potential. Furthermore, selfless people attract other selfless people, causing goodness to cascade throughout their life. In this way, you'll help your players become true difference-makers in the world.

Even though selflessness and emotional intelligence may seem like a natural ability, I believe that people don't learn this skill by happenstance. Instead, it's developed through trial and error, experiences, and mentorship. Your team's sport, whatever it may be, gives your players the opportunity to step outside of themselves, be difference-makers, and be successful in life. Now that's something to be grateful for.

3. **It Goes Beyond the Ball**

Being a part of a team full of different races, ethnicities, and sexual orientations is a true gift that can change a person for the better. This experience will allow them to address different perspectives, injustices, and prejudices, all while learning how to be more accepting.

Our country is incredibly diverse, which is indeed a beautiful thing. Chances are, this diversity is reflected in your team, so not addressing it would be unwise. Instead, use this opportunity to educate, influence, and listen. Your players will gain understanding, empathy, and ultimately leave the world better off than they found it.

Inform your team that this is something to be grateful for. Remind them how fortunate they are to be in a gym or on a field where they can learn perspectives so unlike their own, confront their biases and prejudices, and create diverse friendships. As we all know, the shades of color, ethnicity, sexual orientation, and perspective in this country aren't going anywhere. It's up to everyone to show each other respect and teach this to our youth. When we teach others to look out their windows and listen, they may teach others to do the same. It's a special, but sometimes brutal world, where people are hurting, being brutalized, and are often left behind.

## Gratitude for What We Do

I thank God every day for allowing me to be the head coach of such a young, diverse team. I thank him for my once destructive attachment to basketball, for the times I tried to get my dad's love and attention through it, and because it allowed me to become a coach. And I thank him that I have the opportunity to change the world 12 players at a time.

Remember, like me you were given something bigger too. The beauty of this job is that you can get so much out of it. The joy and exuberance I get from coaching is unmatched—not because I care about playing our rivalries or winning, but because I get to be around a bunch of kids who are just as flawed as I am, and who are trying to be better one day at a time.

Some coaches lecture about the importance of sports because they help teach discipline, accountability, and hard work. These are useful life skills, but they aren't the lessons I'm talking about. For me, it's always been so much deeper than that.

CHAPTER TWELVE

# LOVE BLINDNESS
## POWERING YOUR TEAM TO PLAY THEIR HARDEST

After my brother died, I took a trip to HeartMath Institute in California. He'd asked me to go there with the hope that I would get more in touch with my heart. At the time, that scared the hell out of me, mostly because of my anxiety and panic disorder. Home was my only safe space, and I knew it would be incredibly hard for me to leave. Despite my hesitance, I mustered up the courage to go for my brother's sake.

One plane ride and rental car later, I left the San Jose airport. A bit of time passed on the freeway until I exited and my GPS took me into no man's land. Though the landscape was beautiful, my fears made it hard to appreciate anything in the moment. I weaved through mountains on a precarious highway, bounced around on dirt roads, and got lost a few times before finally finding the institute.

At the welcoming meeting, there were 15 of us. Still emotionally numb and not wanting to be there, I sat down next to a petite woman with shoulder-length brown hair and kind eyes. I jumped when she touched my shoulder.

"I hope this doesn't freak you out, but there's a presence here right now and it's really strong."

I turned toward her. "What do you mean?"

"I'm a medium," she replied with a kind expression. "Your brother died of cancer not too long ago, right? He's here right now, and he's got a big smile on his face. He's so proud of you."

Suddenly, a tidal wave of emotions washed over me. I was confused. I had never met this woman in my life and she was a fellow patron who had no way of knowing why I was there. As I thought about this, I felt his warmth take hold of me too.

Going to HeartMath turned out to be one of the best things I could've done for myself. Not only was I able to connect with my brother, but I was also able to learn about the heart-focused breathing they teach there, which has made its way into my programs. Using this technique for your athletes will allow them to play and live in a way that's connected to the heart, which can help to manage stress and anxiety.

I believe my brother sent me there so I could learn about this life-changing technique, and I hope it will live on with you and your team as well.

## Love as a Tool for Success

If championships are a true measure of success, then the winningest coach in NBA history should indeed be a good source of wisdom. In his book, *Eleven Rings: The Soul of Success,*[20] Phil Jackson speaks highly to the power of love and the vital role it plays in team sports. One of the passages that stuck with me was his discussion of what journalist Sebastian Junger went through when embedded with a platoon of American soldiers in Afghanistan's most dangerous region. While it might seem strange, what Junger discovered amidst the chaos of war was that the courage the soldiers displayed on the battlefield was often indistinguishable from love. This was because of the brotherhoods they formed during extreme hardship, and the willingness to not only fight for each other, but also to put yourself into harm's way to protect the person next to you.

While this type of bond can be difficult to recreate in everyday life, what Jackson and Junger are pointing out here is that it takes the same mentality to succeed in sports. Caring about your teammates and their success above your own selfish desires is key to building the kind of bonds within the team that are necessary to win championships. Of course, there are other factors like talent and luck that play into this equation, but, in the end, none of these things will matter if love isn't the key ingredient.

## Bottle it Up

Coaches always say to me, "Every once in a while, I have a team that has great team chemistry. I wish I could just bottle that up."

The plot twist is, you can! By implementing love into your program, your team will have that *je ne sais quoi* quality. You may find them cracking up in the locker room, or spot them playing on their own in their spare time. You may even find yourself enjoying your job more and don't feel as burnt out. Love has the ability to put another 30 years on your career.

To get started, first you need your athletes to meet their hearts. This beloved exercise is called, "Connecting with the Heart." At first, it may freak your athletes out because it's rather intimate, but they'll eventually learn to love it because it feels great. Before beginning, disclose that they may experience some uncomfortable and/or anxiety-inducing thoughts during the exercise, but request that they follow the rules of mediation and allow the thought to come and go like water. Attempting to shut out the thought will only make it come back.

Next, have the students close their eyes, put a hand over their heart, and visualize breathing in and out *through* the heart. Their inhalation will cause expansion and their exhalation will result in contraction. It should look like the heart is breathing. While they do this for a minute, continue to remind them that their thoughts are going to want to pull them away. Although it may seem counterintuitive at first, they should acknowledge them, accept them, and gently return to their visualization of the heart. Because I always start my day out with this exercise, I know firsthand that the feeling one gets from this is incredible. It's warm and comforting, but strong and inspiring at the same time. It makes you appreciate what you've been given.

To take it to the next level, have your players do one more round, but this time, instruct them to think about something that gives them a feeling of comfort, love, or joy to pump this feeling into the heart. And just to be clear, there's a difference between the *thought* and *feeling* of a memory. We're only looking for the feeling because it's stronger and will better feed the heart.

This new take on the exercise produces an even stronger response in the kids than the first. They will feel more warmth, strength, and security. And most importantly, their love for their heart will grow stronger and stronger. Repeat these exercises as much as you see fit, but make sure to do them at least once a month. If your players like connecting to the heart, they may even request to do it before every practice and game like some of my teams have.

Another great thing to pass on about this training is that everyone can recreate that special feeling whenever they need to, whether it's on the court, before a job interview, a tough conversation, or anytime they're nervous. Because love creates space for forgiveness, listening, and energization, it will conquer all.

## Love in Action

I was forming a new basketball team at our local high school. At the tryouts, it quickly became evident that the most skilled players were freshmen, so I brought all eight of them up to play varsity. Out of this unusually high number, four of them started.

The consensus was that I was crazy for throwing this many freshmen into game action, and that I was going to ruin them and destroy their confidence. I understood this concern, but ultimately ignored it and took pride in the fact that these young players' time on my team wouldn't be about outcomes. Instead, it would be about patience, care, and celebrating who they were growing into as people. But midway through the season, after losing 10 games in a row, it seemed the gossiping parents were going to be right. We were losing in every way possible, sometimes by 25 points and sometimes at the buzzer by two.

Regardless, we never lost hope. Every week, we held a session giving the players space to express how they felt. Many of them were scared, sensed judgment, and dealt with imposter syndrome. We connected to our hearts at least twice a week and before some of our practices. We did appreciation workshops, where they'd discuss wins that had nothing to do with the sport. Everyone helped each other become the best player and person they could be. In my mind, those were the real wins anyway.

In truth, if you had come to a practice without knowing a thing about our record, you would've thought we were having an incredible season based on their work ethic, energy, and how these girls fought for each other. But that didn't change the fact that we finished the regular season with zero wins and 20 loses. Prior to that, I had coached several teams that won conference and district championships, so it would be fair to say that the town was becoming skeptical of me.

However, I wasn't surprised by the team's record. Any other result would've been a miracle. After all, they were 14-year-old girls playing against 17- and 18-year-old players. That made it very difficult for them to compete at the varsity level no matter how talented they were.      I felt a tremendous amount of gratitude for being able to foster an environment of passionate work and purpose that didn't require winning to fuel it. These players understood the bigger picture, and were building relationships with each other based on love.

Since everyone makes it to the playoffs in Michigan, our season didn't end after the regular season. We were lucky enough to be playing one of the highest ranked teams in the state. And unsurprisingly, they crushed us. By a ton of points. I walked into the locker room after the game and found the team huddled in a circle. Everyone was bawling their eyes out. "Why so emotional?" I asked.

Somewhere in the group, a player responded, "Coach, it's not about the loss. It's about missing each other. We want to be at practice tomorrow. We don't want this to end."

With an 0-21 record, they actually felt this way. Have you ever seen a losing team react like that? That's love in action.

The following summer, the players could not wait to get together and start playing again. They *wanted* to play in as many travel tournaments as they could, lift weights, work on agility, and execute speed training. That desire translated to their self-improvement as well. They were motivated by the thought of turning their fortunes around the following season. And most importantly, I didn't have to ask them to do a thing. Their passion and purpose for doing this came from a place of love for each other.

The next season, they accomplished the biggest turnaround in school history by winning 14 games. In the state tournament, they made it to the district final championship game only to lose in a closely contested game to a team that had two D1 players. And they did all of this as sophomores!

Love gives you the energy to persevere, the will to fight, and the ability to overcome the insurmountable odds. Can your team feel it?

# Human Beings

All teams will at some point experience pain and anguish. You haven't opened your eyes yet or are unwilling to if you don't recognize this. That's why this sentiment I've heard from some coaches deeply concerns me: *I'm not going to change a thing as long as we're playing well. I don't want to mess with anything.*

Chances are that someone in that locker room is in pain and is hurting. There will be someone on the bench who feels alone. Discounting these truths will rot the team from the inside out, and your team will be worse off for it. Ignorance is the silent cause of drain, burnout, and division.

I remember avoiding this reality for a long time. One day, I finally asked my brother, "How do you know it's there? How can you be so sure?"

"Because, Patrick," he replied. "We're human beings. Show me a person that hasn't experienced some kind of pain and I'll tell you they're not human."

# Setting Up for Success

Now that you're aware of the importance of love, let me explain how you can cement it into your program. In a general sense, you should:

- Set up plenty of opportunities to connect to the heart. The teams we work with at Elite Performance Too-E do this exercise before many of their practices and for an extended time twice a month. It's necessary for love—the most important teaching of all—to exist.

- Do the belonging exercise a few times during the season to set up opportunities to express who they are outside of the sport (e.g. What's your family like? What stresses you out? What do you love doing?). We've touched on this concept before. Having a sense of belonging is critical to being able to feel and share love. You want your players to be able to express their authentic selves to their teammates. It will allow them to identify with each other. Common interests will draw them closer, and love will spread amongst the team like wildfire.

- You must interact with your staff with the same love and respect you give to your players. Your players are watching you even when you don't think they are. You can't fool them. They'll notice if you aren't treating your colleagues the same way you're treating them, which will cause them to lose faith in the love you're giving them. But regardless of the above justification, you should treat your staff with kindness because of the simple fact that they're human too, and it's the right thing to do.

- Integrate the word love into your messaging. There's an art to saying the word *love* authentically. Unlike the rest of the information in this book, this cannot be taught. If you don't mean it when you say it to these kids, you should probably be doing something else.

When you do finally break past that barrier of discomfort and add *love* into your sentences, the power of it can be incredible. For example, I coached a troubled high school basketball team with a tough exterior. Based on their demeanors and attitudes, I guessed some of them had never heard the word at home.

Day after day, I showered them in it. I said things like, "I love coaching this team, and I love you guys so much. There's nowhere I'd rather be right now. You need to know that" during timeouts, practices, and games. But for a long time, I got nothing back.

The sixth game was a rough one, and so during a timeout I got on them a little bit. "There's nothing you guys could say or do to make me not want to be here. The amount of wins we get has no effect on how much I love you guys. I know you will grow up to be great men."

One of the kids shot up and hugged me so hard it nearly killed me. Then they told me they loved me and thanked me. Love was changing these men, and that's why I do what I do.

Finally, below is a specific exercise you can follow to the tee if you don't know where to start. This drill will highlight all the ways love is already in your athletes' lives.

1. Have your players write down three people they love in their lives on a piece of paper.

2. Tell them to elaborate why they love these people.

3. Break the players down in small groups and have them share what they wrote down.

4. Bring the entire team back together. Instruct each group to share one or two examples. Then, ask what they learned.

5. Break the team back into their groups. Ask the groups to collaborate and come up with five action steps that will allow the team to build love.

6. Bring the team back together. Tell each group to share their five action steps and write them on the whiteboard.

7. Lastly, have the entire team collaborate to pick five. Post these somewhere in your locker room as a reminder of what's required of them.

And there you have it. These tips should guide you towards implementing love in the foundation of your team.

## Kevin Knew

One day, while Kevin and I were grabbing lunch, Kevin stopped digging into his Greek salad and said, "Why are you always up in your head?" I stopped chewing out of surprise, then waited for him to say more. "It's just that—during so many of our conversations, I see your brain turning to measure the next few sentences. When are you going to go to your heart?"

I didn't know it at the time, but part of my emptiness was rooted in my lack of connection to my heart. If you were to point to something that defines you, without exception, you would point to your heart. This means I was ignoring the biggest part of my authentic self.

If that's the place that defines us, why do we shut it off all the time? You can't build love from *Xs* and *Os*. At the same time, you will never be fulfilled without it. You can lift a trophy in celebration, read about your victory in the papers, and get congratulations from your peers. While that's all wonderful, it won't last. It'll only force you to continue reaching for the next thing to get that elation, almost like a drug.

As humans, we're constantly searching for something to fill a void or to get us through the day. But love is free, and your heart was given to you. It's something that has the ability to change your life that already exists within us. So, if you can only take one teaching away from this book, choose love. The rest will follow.

Also remember that you're blessed enough to have the opportunity to create a space where people can truly understand one another. When you do that, kids will naturally want to compete because they love being with each other, and this will have nothing to do with the outcome.

# CHAPTER THIRTEEN

# THE COACH'S HANDBOOK
## HOW TO BECOME A BETTER COACH

In my time doing this line of work through Elite Performance Too-E, I've learned a great deal of things that have ultimately made me a better coach and person. Next, I will outline the tenets that have changed my life in the hopes that they will change yours too.

1. **I'm not your friend.**

   Personally, I think this is old school thinking. A head coach must invest meaningful time connecting with their players on a personal level.

   One weekend, I was watching Gavin O'Connor's 2004 film *Miracle*, which follows the USA ice hockey team that beat the Russians during their journey towards winning gold. The movie gives us a look into the profile of head coach Herb Brooks, whose own ice hockey career culminated in him being cut from the U.S. Olympic team when he was a player just before the Olympics. That moment would affect him forever.

At the end of tryouts, Brooks gathered his potential players together so he could read off the roster. Standing across from the players in the bleachers, he went through each name one by one until he was done. After the players who didn't make it left, he made a statement to those who were selected. "I'll be your coach. I won't be your friend. If you need one of those, take it up with Doc or Coach Patrick here."[21] And then, he left the rink.

When he said that, a lightbulb went off in my head as I remembered *this* was where that prevalent saying comes from. Obviously, things worked out for Coach Brooks even though he had an "I'm not your friend" mentality. But I do think that many players today require more collaboration, co-creating, and personal connection to help them tap into their own passion and purpose for competing. It's time we adapt.

Perhaps one of the biggest ways we can do that is by being willing to personally connect with your players. Connecting, to me, means making an effort to have interactions with them that aren't related to their sport. What are their struggles? What are their challenges? What brings them joy?

You may or may not have good chemistry with them, but that's not what matters. What matters is that you're displaying a willingness to bond with them and are showing them you care. When you do that, there's a greater chance that they'll give you their best possible selves. Some of the benefits you may experience from leaving the "I am not your friend" mentality behind will be an increase in your team's athletic performance and an increase in personal joy, energy, and excitement related to your sport. The connection you have with your team will show your investment in them and make you want to do more for them. This will put an immeasurable amount of time on your coaching career. It's not that things like drills, film, and training won't still feel time consuming, but instead doing them just won't feel like drudgery as much as it might otherwise.

Some may say having this approach to coaching is garbage because you'll lose respect. To that, I would say you are behind the times. I've found that todays' athletes want collaboration, inclusion, and a more personal connection to their coaches. If this kind of environment isn't created, the level of trust between coach and player will suffer.

While I'm evidently against the "I am not your friend" mentality, I want to be clear that I also don't think you should be their best friend either. There has to be balance and boundaries. While you can connect deeply with your players, they should still see you as a coach. It's about living in the gray area, not seeing things as just black or white.

Although my athletes and I get along well, they know when I'm being serious, feeling disappointed, or think something is unacceptable. They respond to me with the kind of respect that every coach deserves. At the same time, they know I'm not perfect because I've demonstrated to them time and time again that I'm not—and that's really the key to all of this. I don't pretend to have all the answers or be perfect. As the coach and leader of the program, one of my primary responsibilities is to continuously search for ways to connect with my players and to influence and motivate them to become the best version of themselves.

The title comes with a lot of opacity, so you're going to have to define it for yourself, just as I did. To begin, I would direct you to the workshops shared in this book. They will enable you to establish the personal connections required to make a difference. I recommend the intimacy workshop as a go to.

2. **Coaches need to make an intentional commitment towards integrating, developing, and building intrinsic connections within players and coaches.**

The second action required for you to become a better coach is to put in the work required by developing compassion, gratitude, belonging, love, trust, and integrity. I can imagine this is where you, the reader, may get a little stuck if you've never done this kind of work. You know everything I teach through Elite Performance Too-E, but it can be extremely confusing to formulate and develop a strategy alone.

To combat this, I focus on workshops like compassion, gratitude, belonging, love, trust, and integrity first. All of these skills are powerful because they create a strong foundation of ideals on your team and an athletic experience that's unique and distinct from other programs.

But before you do that, show this to your team:

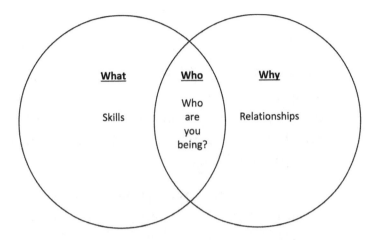

In the first session, I always put this illustration up on the board and point to the *What* and explain that it represents *the skill*. Most will easily relate to this one, identifying that it contains drills, exercises, execution, and shooting. This realm is full of entirely extrinsic goals. At this point, I tell them, "If I had skilled players that just did *What* 95% of the time, we would probably win. But there's something bigger going on that I want to awaken you guys to."

That leads me to the two intrinsic commitments, with the first being the *Why, the passion and purpose.* When I ask my players to write down what their passion and purpose is, I often get responses like, *winning a state championship,* or *I love basketball.* I tell them that *Why* is deeper than that. It's the reason you continue to play when adversity hits the hardest, when mental fatigue sets in, and when you feel like you have nothing else left to give. Honestly, winning or having love for the sport isn't enough for most people—especially when a team isn't having success.

*Why* counteracts that and is the catalyst.

To get started, I normally give them a hint in the form of a question. "What's the most significant gift you're receiving by being part of this team?" In all the time I've done this kind of work, I've never received the answer I'm looking for, which is the relationships.

When you're on a team, you begin to establish these very intentional connections to each other and formulate this idea that the most significant thing you bring to the team is your ability to help others reach their best possible selves. When you go into a locker room, out into the corridor, or compete with these people, the drive to help them is what keeps you going. When you're tired, when you're losing, or hitting adversity, if your passion and purpose has that kind of meaning, you'll have the ability to respond and overcome.

Usually, they'll respond that they had no idea relationships were the most significant gift, and I'll say, "Think about it. It's not a coincidence that your 12 teammates are sitting next to each other. I want you to wake up to the fact that you were all brought together for a purpose, for the opportunity to change someone's life. That's what's going to fuel you instead of the outcomes and accolades."

That's the *Why*, but the second intrinsic commitment is the *Who*—and it happens to be the most important one. The question here is, *Who* are you being when you're doing the *What* and you're executing the *Why?* What is your attitude and behavior? What are the things that you need to work on? What are your shortcomings?

The *Who* is the most interrelated facet of the diagram because it's directly tied to identity. A player cannot do the *What* (skills) or the *Why* (relationships) to the best of their ability if their *Who* isn't developed. When all three of them work together in tandem, the athlete will be unstoppable.

Knowing that, if you want to become a better coach, you need to change the way you approach your sport. Most coaches work on just the *What* approximately 80% to 90% of the time, but it needs to be more holistic than that. At minimum at least 25% of your program should be spent on the *Why* and *Who*.

3.  **Take a fearless and honest inventory to identify your personal and coaching shortcomings and strengths. Celebrate your strengths but be willing to execute H.O.W. as it applies to your shortcomings.**

    Can you take it? Do you have the courage to do this? I know it's tough to perform something like H.O.W. or any of the other exercises on yourself, but I believe that a coach needs to be fearless enough to do an honest inventory of themselves and look at their shortcomings, both personal and as a coach. After all, how can you expect your team to be brave enough to work on themselves if you don't do the same?

I think it's important that we as coaches humble ourselves through these exercises because we think we have so much to teach. But in reality, players are usually the ones who teach us more about ourselves than we teach them. And so, if we're willing to be present and willing to be humble, you can't help but improve and become better—not only as a coach, but as a person.

4. **Use outside resources if necessary to help influence, build, and mentor excellence.**

A lot of coaches have trouble passing the torch to someone else. Whether it's trust or ego, it makes sense that a coach wouldn't want to have just anybody come into their program. The truth is the harm an outside party could do is minimal in comparison to the change and insight they can potentially provide.

Think about it. You're just one person and there's no way you can speak to the experiences of every single person on your team. Instead, bring in a person that can teach your players (and you) when something becomes too overwhelming or foreign for you to handle. It doesn't mean that you're any less capable, as every person has their threshold and specialties.

For example, I brought in Tre' Gammage because I thought he could make an impact on everyone—especially our Black players, because I'm White and cannot speak to their experience. Some people you could reach out to are motivational speakers, life coaches, community leaders, charities, sports figures, and other coaches. Above all else, don't be afraid to ask for help.

5.  **Be approachable. If players know you authentically care about who they are as people, they won't hold back from sharing personal struggles and challenges they're dealing with. This builds an intimate connection.**

If you want to be a better coach, you have to let your players know that they can come to you with absolutely anything. You do that by letting down your guard and understanding your position in their lives.

Similar to number one, I'm not suggesting you become friends with your players. Instead, I'm suggesting you learn to create human bonds with them and to function and exist on a level that's separate from any kind of stereotypical role. Being approachable makes you into a better coach because as you grow personally, there's more room for you to develop a stronger connection to your players. Otherwise, you'll put up armor to protect yourself.

On the other hand, if your team knows you authentically care about who they are, they won't hold back from sharing their personal struggles and challenges. This will allow you to build an intimate connection and foundation of trust.

To go about this, ask yourself questions like these:

- What have I shared?

- What are some of the actions I'm taking?

- What are some of the steps that I'm taking to demonstrate I'm an approachable person?

- How am I establishing that atmosphere?

- How am I interacting with my players beyond basketball?

- What am I asking them about their day and life?

Let down your guard and let your players in.

6. **Acquire enough humility to take feedback from your players about your attitude, behavior, and actions as a person.**

   This is another area where you can learn as much from your players as they can learn from you. Be humble, present, open, and vulnerable. Encourage your players to be honest with you and let you know when you exhibit behaviors that might cause friction and hurt the team. Some things are obviously not up for debate or a vote. However, even those things will be better received from your players if they know that you're open and fair when considering ideas or suggestions from them. When you do this, you can't help but become a better coach and person.

7. **Work toward expressing vulnerability to demonstrate that you are human.**

   When you're vulnerable with others, especially people that don't expect it, you're really communicating that you're human. You can do this by sharing personal stories, your demons, and your likes and dislikes.

   Vulnerability's most significant benefit is that it builds trust, and when players trust their coach, they're more honest with them. I believe that honest communication, when occurring from all parties, creates a domino effect on a program and improves all aspects. This is especially true because it challenges a coach to reflect on their teachings and behavior.

Please note that you shouldn't consider being vulnerable in order to be saved by the players. That's a form of manipulation. Instead of you giving something to them, you're taking something from them because they're making *you* feel better. They're being the generous ones in that situation, not you.

Alternatively, being vulnerable is being able to say, *This is what I've experienced, and this is who I am*, while simultaneously articulating that you've got everything taken care of in your life, even if you're dealing with a lot of pain. For instance, when I told my team about the abortions, I didn't ask them to do anything for me. I wasn't even expecting the reaction I got.

Just remember, it's impossible to know how to motivate a player to their fullest capacity if you only know them from a surface level. People are complicated, which is why it's always better to get to know people on more than just a surface level. Vulnerability takes every relationship to an entirely different depth, allowing for more passion, more purpose, and an unrelenting fire to not let each other down.

8. **Develop, introduce, and commit to helping players become more consciously aware of all the benefits being part of a team provides. Create a list of things they should be grateful for and bring great value that has**

**nothing to do with playing time. Do not assume they already know them.**

Becoming a better coach manifests itself when you're not being dragged down by all the other things that can occur when you're leading a team such as drama, clashes, and politics. Friction of this kind affects you as a coach as well as the entire team.

If you try to manage every one of these problems as they pop up, you will fail. There will be simply too many that are too complex, and you won't have enough time to solve. However, there's a way to respond to drama that limits the number of issues that arise.

For me, gratitude is the antidote. You must help your team understand the value of being a part of something bigger than themselves. When one is a part of a team, they're going to have an opportunity to learn skills that will benefit them for the rest of their lives. This includes being cooperative, forming bonds, and building emotional intelligence.

If you can do that, you'll become a better coach because you can spend your time where it's needed instead of dealing with frustration, displeasure, selfishness, and division. And, like Kevin always said, don't think you can just sweep friction amongst your team under the carpet and pretend it doesn't exist or have an impact. Free yourself by freeing them first.

9. **It's not about you, your ego, or pursing personal accolades to feed your insecurities. You've been given the**

**awesome responsibility of influencing and connecting with players to help them handle life. You partake in forming their core values, common decency, ability to think outside of themselves, and the willingness to pay it forward.**

If you're motivated by coaching and want to truly impact others in a meaningful way, then you understand there's so much more to coaching than just winning itself. The greatest coaches in the world have been the ones that were impactful, empathetic, and life changing. Winning is only a byproduct of that.

When I realized it wasn't about me or my ego, I was able to draw the conclusion that winning wasn't the only thing. Instead, I recognized the awesome responsibility that had been given to me by these young men and women. When I came to that conclusion, I became a better, more humble coach.

In a similar vein, working on the *Why* and the *Who* isn't for you. You owe it to the players because they haven't grown up in a time that's been very forgiving, generous, or gracious to them. They've grown up in a world where it's better to be selfish, individualistic, and self-serving. Even if you can't do a minimum of 25% of the intrinsic like I suggest, how about you just *try* 10%?

Like I said, you owe it to them, yourself, and the world. Ultimately, the biggest way you can become a better coach is by making your players better people.

CHAPTER FOURTEEN

# THE STAGES OF CHANGE

I got a call the other day from a school I've worked with for a long time. It was one of the ones Kevin asked me to continue doing work for.

"Patrick, it's just amazing," I heard in my ear. "This team used to have no passion, but now they're teeming with it. Now I know that it has to be taught and reinforced again and again."

As you move through the lessons offered in this book, you should start to notice a certain evolution in your team that indicates they are on track. In this chapter, I'll point out those stages and use examples from my team's journey. My hope is that you, like me, will notice an incredible transformation in your team.

1. **The Starting Point**

    Assess where your team currently stands. What shape is your program in? What are its weaknesses, and your strong points? Is your team broken? I know mine was. To give you perspective, when I was asked to be a coach, the team had seven losing seasons in a row under its belt and only nine winning seasons in the past 37 years. The program lacked consistent success as far as wins and losses and weren't winning in the emotional department either.

Behavioral problems came and went like seasons. The year before I became coach, many players either quit the team or were kicked off of it. There was everything from talking back, detentions and fighting, to walking off the floor in the middle of practice. Ultimately, there was a high degree of selfishness and lack of understanding of the team concept. Also, many of them were carrying these issues into the classroom and failing academically.

## 2. **The Foundation**

That was what I came into, and the first thing I did was figure out where to begin. Walking into the gym on the first day of practice, I wasn't surprised to see everyone avoid eye contact when I introduced myself—which is why I immediately felt that we needed to start by developing trust. And again, the only lasting way I knew to build trust was primarily through vulnerability.

I gathered all the players for a session. The entire time I spoke to them, they couldn't look me in the eye. There was such a lack of trust, such a strong fear of connecting, that they wouldn't even allow themselves to try and be open. But I wasn't about to be one of the many coaches that quit on them.

When I did the vulnerability exercise, I decided to frame it as an opportunity for the players to get to know me, rather than expect anything out of them. I shared some of my experiences that were personal to me, telling them that I thought it was important to talk about who I was as a person, not a coach, so they could have a meaningful relationship with me. I invited them to ask questions or share if they felt compelled to do so, but the room remained quiet and their eyes stayed glued to the floor.

Still, I wasn't thrown by it. I didn't get angry, scream at them, or force them to look at me. All I saw were a bunch of kids who were hurting and understandably didn't trust me. As we went on with practices, I continued to hold vulnerability sessions and share my experiences growing up as a boy in an abusive and impoverished household. I talked about my demons, alcoholism, self-loathing, hate, panic, and anxiety disorder.

And then something happened. Slowly but surely, the heads began to rise. I know this may seem like a small gesture, but it was huge. It told me we were finally making progress. By demonstrating that I didn't have all the answers, that I was human and that life happens to coaches too turned out to be very effective, since it wasn't something they weren't used to hearing. If I'd tried to demand that kind of good behavior from them, lecture them, or set rules to abide by, I would've failed miserably.

Instead, they raised their heads.

### 3.  Time for Some Hard Work

As time passed, my team and I slowly built trust, safety, and a more intimate connection with each other. This is what should occur for you after stage two. I continued to do vulnerability exercises with them but branched out into other ones to give them a well-rounded experience.

Bit by bit, I began to see changes in their behavior. Some players started to share in the sessions, while others came up to me individually and said hello when I entered the gym. Once I felt they were comfortable enough with me, I decided to move to the next step. Now it was time to do the H.O.W. session with them.

I explained the exercise first, then used myself and my experiences as an example, talking about all the things I use H.O.W. to work on every day to improve myself. As I wrapped up, I stated, "I have shortcomings. I'm 60 years old, but I'm just like you. I'm not a perfect person, and neither are you. But that's okay. I'll be working on these issues and I give all of you permission to hold me accountable to that. I won't take it as a threat or as being disrespectful. I won't take it as anything other than you guys trying to help me become a better person, and for that I'd be grateful."

I turned to face them and concluded by saying, "Would you guys be willing to look at some of your own short-comings with the thought of helping each other grow as people?" I then asked them to write their shortcomings down. Some of the common struggles were not being coachable, being angry, being disrespectful to each other, quitting on themselves, and having poor grades.

After we went through their answers, I asked each of them to consider giving me and their teammates permission to hold them accountable. I also asked them to have great patience because these habits weren't going to change overnight. They all agreed to it.

I laugh about it now, but for the next two weeks, all my coaching staff and I did was point out when our player's shortcomings came up. Sometimes it wouldn't require a stern voice, and other times it would. But even then, it was never a lecture. We always asked for permission to point them out.

Unfortunately, this was the stage where we had to let a few players go—specifically the ones who refused to buy in, be held accountable, and change. One of them was one of our best players who was an all-conference player. We left some of those players in tears, but those tears represented important progress. We hoped to help them learn a valuable lesson, and furthermore, it served the dual purpose of proving to the rest of the team that we were serious about our program's philosophy.

The sad reality of the situation is that I suspect these players were left heartbroken, as it may have been the first time, they actually had to pay a price for their attitudes and behaviors. They loved to play and it was being taken away from them.

When a coach is committed to loving each player, it's truly gut wrenching to dismiss a player from the team. In fact, I've had many sleepless nights spent thinking about whether to dismiss a player or not. My hope is always that their dismissal from the team will be a lesson that makes them own up to their destructive attitudes and behaviors. That they will become willing to change, not for the benefit of basketball, but for their lives. In this instance, I felt it reached a point where I could only do the right thing by taking them off the court.

Only time will tell if any impact was made, but it's worth even if only a seed was planted.

4. **What's the Bigger Picture?**

After five months of doing the hard work, we went from a team that couldn't make eye contact to a team that committed to work on their destructive behaviors. That change alone is almost a miracle. And it only happened because they trusted me.

Once you've built enough trust between you and your team to do the hard work (i.e., do challenging exercises, go deeply personal, form real relationships), you can begin to focus your attention on finding the bigger picture. So, what do I mean by that? The bigger picture starts to take shape when you make your players aware of the purpose beyond the orange ball. It happens when they understand that outcomes don't matter and that who they are as human beings is far more important than any scoreboard.

When I first told my team this, they asked me, "What could possibly be bigger than wanting to win? What could be bigger than conference championships, state championships, or awards?" And when I asked what the gifts of the game were, they were stumped. They didn't come close to recognizing how special the relationships they were building were.

At that moment, I knew if I couldn't get them to shift that mindset we were never going to win if we didn't have heart. That's when we started doing workshops on subjects like belonging, selflessness, and gratitude. My players needed to learn about each other as people and appreciate everything the game was teaching them about life. Through those exercises, we taught our players to embrace everything being presented to them because of this game. Through passion, purpose, and understanding, they learned that basketball isn't just about winning—it's about being selfless and forming relationships. Excellence has to be in everything we do, whether it be as a player, person, student, son, daughter, boyfriend, girlfriend, or anything else.

And all of a sudden, even though we were losing, I knew we weren't going to fall apart. At the time, we had two wins and 16 loses late into the season. Even though we were losing a lot, every single person was working their ass off, and their effort was a breath of fresh air. This team wasn't fighting with each other anymore or slamming lockers when they got angry. This team actually loved each other.

The concept that took them the longest to grasp was selflessness. But when they started playing games with the goal of helping their teammates become the best they can be, we became very competitive—seemingly out of the blue. Suddenly we were competing at a high level and beating a few teams that we had no right to be on the floor with. On the court, my players started to help their teammates, chose to pass instead of keeping the glory, and communicated like never before. Off the court, they began to assist each other with classroom work, get lunch together, and hang out as friends.

That was all possible because we introduced them to the bigger picture and because they became aware of the things to be grateful for. Above all else, they learned how to fight for each other.

5. **The Oasis**

We had 35 kids and nine coaches from highly successful programs that wanted to come be a part of what we're doing. The year before our staff was hired to run the program there were many players who quit playing, along with the entire coaching staff stepping down. But even though we have more players this year, we're still a losing team. So, why are they coming? Because the name is the same, but the program is different. There's a connection to the players that runs much deeper. There's care and love and lots of important lessons being taught.

This is how I know we've reached *the oasis*. That, however, doesn't mean the work is done. One of my main focuses right now is to get the team to be academically independent of the basketball program. A lot of our players only get Cs because they want to play basketball instead of being internally motivated by something else.

The other day, three of our seniors voted with the team, and everyone agreed. No one is allowed to carry anything less than a letter grade of C. Any player with a letter grade lower than C will have to go to study hall with another player that will help them get there. The team decided this on their own.

A year ago, we had to figure out who was going to be academically suspended and who wasn't every week. Now I get texts from players that say, *Coach, look at my grades. I'm proud of them!*

My players, like yours, just need somebody to believe in them. Someone that truly loves them, cares for them, and is willing to teach them what's most important in life. This also includes being patient with them, firm, and explaining disappointment when it's required. This is not just a program. Instead, it's an example of what a program can become. And it all happened in a year.

## The Stages of Change

These are the stages of change. You have to trust, be vulnerable, be vulnerable *again*, and then ask them to be vulnerable back. As time passes and you notice an evolution, learn to trust your gut. As a coach, if you know your players and you'll know when they're ready to be challenged emotionally.

During this process, remember that you're learning and have shortcomings of your own. Know that you're asking them to help you grow too. I've used my example because it's an extreme one that shows how effective these philosophies can be. Just keep in mind that your team doesn't have to be this bankrupt. Even if your team is doing great on the surface, things can always be better. These boys and girls are starving for these kinds of lessons, and it's our job to give it to them.

# CHAPTER FIFTEEN

# YOU ARE ENOUGH

When my brother passed on his work to me all those years ago, it wasn't the only gift he gave me. With those bright, crystal blue eyes and his peaceful expression, Kevin looked up at me and said, "Patrick, I want you to be happy and content. And I want you to know that you're a very special man." Gently, he took my hand and squeezed it. "You're enough."

I froze for a moment to process what I'd just heard. There I was, a 55-year-old man who thought I had everything figured out, and that going to therapy would fix me. I thought being sober for 25 years and having money would fix me. But nothing ever filled the dark void inside of me that years of abuse left. And yet, my brother's words made me realize that I didn't need to be fixed. I became whole knowing that I wasn't perfect, and that everything I'd suffered made me the opposite of unlovable.

I burst into tears because my brother was so close to passing and I knew he had no motive other than love. Even more incredible was the fact that *he* was the one suffering, and I was supposed to be the one there for him. Even in his final moments, he couldn't stop giving to others.

After I left my brother's home, I was finally able to find comfort for the first time in my life. It took a lot of time and hard work, but I can tell you I'm now a person who loves themselves unconditionally and I'm proud of myself for surviving everything that was thrown my way.

I also don't feel the need to prove anything in order to feel loved and worthy. Ever since then, I've carried his presence with me everywhere I go. My brother is a part of everything I do and will be forever. I feel him every time I walk into the gym, talk to one of my athletes, and pass on his message. This is why he's such a big part of this book too. It's because of him that I've learned to be present, listen to those around me, and work to be just as impactful as he was. Today, I'm also more open to different ideas and don't feel the need to prove that I'm right or know better.

The completeness he gave me is ultimately the biggest gift I can share with my athletes and with every life that I touch. I try to make everyone aware of the fact that they are special, loved, and enough. This involves you, too. I truly mean it when I say *you are enough*. Just like Kevin left me with a mission, I'm going to leave one with you before we part. It's up to you to continue his work.

I'm only one person, but together, I truly believe we can change things for the better. My hope is that the tools, workshops, and tenets you've been given through this book give you the ability to do just that. The time is now, and you have the potential to do something great with your life, to make a real difference, and to do good. Not many people are given that opportunity. *It's up to you to embrace this gift you've been given.*

# ACKNOWLEDGMENTS

I want to thank Coach Tim Gushue and Coach Don Green from Shawnee High School, Coach Tim McAneney and Joe Wojceichowski from Lenape High School, Coach Josh Hood from Brandywine High School, Coach Jesse Brown from United Football, Coach Maureen Brown from Kalamazoo Valley Community College, and Nan Carney-Debord, Athletic Director from Denison University for trusting in my work, which allowed me the opportunity to apply the lessons from the book.

I want to thank my high school basketball coaches, Coach Roger Kindle (deceased), and Coach Joe Lafferty. Both of these men planted a seed of hope inside of me, which eventually inspired me to believe I could change the course of abuse and hardship from which I was raised.

I want to thank Barry McDonagh, Michelle Cavanaugh, and the entire DARE family. The strength, courage, confidence, and unconditional love I received from them while producing this book were immeasurable.

I want to thank all of the athletes who trusted me enough to do the courageous work required within this book. I am the one who is blessed to have crossed paths with each of them.

Finally, I would like to thank the family at Book Launchers. Without their guidance, experience, expertise, encouragement, and positivity, this book would not have been possible.

# ENDNOTES

1   Ben Shumate, "30 Percent of Athletes Quit Respective Teams," The Brown Daily Herald, April 28, 2016, https://www.browndailyherald.com/2016/04/28/30-percent-of-athletes-quit-respective-teams/.

2   Ema Schumer, "One in Four Class of 2020 Athletes Quit Varsity Teams During Their Time at Harvard," The Harvard Crimson, February 21, 2020, https://www.thecrimson.com/article/2020/2/21/athlete-attrition-data-2020/.

3   Brian Hainline, Lydia Bell, and Mary Wilfert, "Mind, Body and Sport: Substance Use and Abuse," NCAA, accessed August 3, 2021, https://www.ncaa.org/sport-science-institute/mind-body-and-sport-substance-use-and-abuse.

4   Mary Elizabeth, "Abuse of Prescription Painkillers on the Rise Among High School Athletes: Survey," US News, August 4, 2014, https://health.usnews.com/health-news/articles/2014/08/04/abuse-of-prescription-painkillers-on-the-rise-among-high-school-athletes-survey.

5   Linda Flanagan, "Why Are So Many Teen Athletes Struggling With Depression?," The Atlantic, April 17, 2019, https://www.theatlantic.com/education/archive/2019/04/teen-athletes-mental-illness/586720/.

6   "Statistics and Research on Eating Disorders," National Eating Disorders Association, May 8, 2020, https://www.nationaleatingdisorders.org/statistics-research-eating-disorders.

7   Kelly Wallace, "From '80s latchkey kid to helicopter parent today," CNN Health, March 30, 2016, https://www.cnn.com/2016/03/30/health/the-80s-latchkey-kid-helicopter-parent/index.html.

8   Sally C. Curtin, Holly Hedegaard, Arialdi Minino, Margaret Warner, and Thomas Simon, "QuickStats: Suicide Rates for Teens Aged 15–19 Years, by Sex — United States, 1975–2015," Centers for Disease Control and Prevention (CDC), August 4, 2017, https://www.cdc.gov/mmwr/volumes/66/wr/mm6630a6.htm.

9   Holly B. Shakya and Nicholas A. Christakis, "Association of Facebook Use with Compromised Well-Being: A Longitudinal Study," American Journal of Epidemiology 185, no. 3 (2017), https://doi.org/10.1093/aje/kww189.

10  "Sexual Violence is Preventable," CDC, accessed August 3, 2021, https://www.cdc.gov/injury/features/sexual-violence/index.html.

11  Seventy-One Percent of Employers Say They Value Emotional Intelligence over IQ, According to CareerBuilder Survey," Career Builder, August 18, 2011, https://www.careerbuilder.ca/share/aboutus/pressreleasesdetail.aspx?id=pr652&sd=8%2f18%2f2011&ed=8%2f18%2f2099.

12  "Participation in High School Sports Registers First Decline in 30 Years," National Federation of State High School Associations (NFHS), September 5, 2019, https://www.nfhs.org/articles/participation-in-high-school-sports-registers-first-decline-in-30-years/.

13  "Motivational Quotes," Coach John Wooden: Pyramid of Success, accessed August 3, 2021, https://www.thewoodeneffect.com/motivational-quotes/.

14  John Wooden and Jay Carty, Coach Wooden's Pyramid of Success (Ada, MI: Revell, 2009).

15  "Penn Commencement 2011: Fall Forward," University of Pennsylvania Almanac 57, no. 34 (2011), https://almanac.upenn.edu/archive/volumes/v57/n34/comm-washington.html.

16  "Youth Sports Facts: Sports Participation and Physical Activity Rates," Project Play, https://www.aspenprojectplay.org/youth-sports-facts/participation-rates.

17  Jacob Bogage, "Youth Sports Study: Declining Participation, Rising Costs and Unqualified Coaches," The Washington Post, September 6, 2017, https://www.washingtonpost.com/news/recruiting-insider/wp/2017/09/06/youth-sports-study-declining-participation-rising-costs-and-unqualified-coaches/

18  "Youth Sports Facts: Challenges to Physical Activity."

19  Tory Higgins, Shared Reality: What Makes Us Strong and Tears Us Apart (Oxford, UK: Oxford University Press, 2019).

20  Phil Jackson and Hugh Delehanty, Eleven Rings: The Soul of Success (New York, NY: Penguin, 2004).

21  Miracle, dir. Gavin O'Connor (1994), Walt Disney/Mayhem Pictures/Buena Vista, 136 mins.